THE FAITH THAT REBELS

THE FAITH THAT REBELS

A Re-examination of the Miracles of Jesus

D. S. CAIRNS

SCM PRESS LTD
56 BLOOMSBURY STREET
LONDON

To

H. W. C.

First published 1928
Second edition 1928
Third edition 1929
Fourth edition 1930
Fifth edition 1933
Sixth edition 1954

Printed in Great Britain by
Billing and Sons Limited Guildford and London

CONTENTS

FOREWORD

I was extremely glad when I learned that it was proposed to issue a new edition of this very notable book, and I gladly responded to the invitation to write a foreword which would introduce it to a new generation of readers. This is one of the books that have influenced me greatly and permanently in the never-ending endeavour to think out our Christian faith. At the time when it first appeared, I had, like many others, been looking forward with some eagerness to its publication, for we knew that Cairns had for a long time been saying to his students at Aberdeen something new and enlivening on the subject of faith and miracles, and a savour of it was sometimes borne to us on a wind from the north. I read the book at once, and even if its argument did not carry me with it all the way, I have ever since then regarded it as a book which made me see something that I had not seen before and which must be important for my understanding of Christianity. Probably many others of my generation could say the same. The reviewer of the first edition in the *Guardian* wrote: " At last we have a book on miracles which really moves the problem out of the stalemate into which it had fallen. . . . This is a book of first-rate apologetic importance and value which may mark a definite step forward in the treatment of this ancient issue." I believe that it did.

A great deal has happened in the theological world since the nineteen-twenties, and the landscape has been transformed more than in most periods of that length. I have sometimes wondered whether, amid a wealth of new insights from new angles, the particular insight which Cairns's book helped to create in the understanding of the Gospels is in some quarters being lost or forgotten. Theology today in its approach to the miracle-stories in the Gospels is apt to be primarily interested in asking: What significance had these stories in the preaching of the early Church out of which the Gospels grew? To what "forms" do they belong in the tradition that was taking shape? What light do they throw upon the nature and content of the apostolic *kerygma*? And what will a truly "biblical" theology (as distinguished from a merely historical interest) have to say about them? These are indeed important questions. And Cairns was not blind to them. His theology was biblical through and through, and the reading of his books makes one exclaim: "How that man knows and understands the Bible, both Old and New Testaments!" Moreover, he is greatly concerned to show that "mighty works" are part of the very *content* of the message of the early Church. But he is even more concerned with the questions (which to him are inseparable from the foregoing, and are not unanswerable): How did our Lord Himself regard His "mighty works"? What did He hold and teach about the possibility of such things happening? Did they really happen? And if they did, was this something entirely exceptional, confined to the lives of our Lord and His apostles, and perhaps a few great saints throughout the ages, as "miracle-workers" whose exploits were intended to confirm the Christian message? Or is this an integral and permanent part of the message itself, a part often lost from the Church in the past, but now being rediscovered and realized in the faith-healing movements of our time?

To Cairns these questions were vital. In his student days he had passed through a period of agonizing doubt about Christianity, and it was partly through eager study of the Gospels in the light of modern criticism, and especially of the Kingdom of God in the New Testament, that he found his way back to faith. Thus to him the miracles were the mighty works of the Kingdom of God, wrought by the power of God made available through human faith, of which Jesus himself was "the pioneer and perfection." Moreover, this whole subject was in Cairns's mind closely connected with his own experience, when, after only a few years of married life, his young wife contracted an illness which finally carried her away. He was thus driven to face the problem of the meaning and conquest of suffering and death, so prominent in the New Testament. At the same time, though he was not a scientist, he was deeply interested in the developments of modern science, moving away so remarkably from the materialist-mechanistic world-view which had been so widespread and so intimidating. And he had also a profound interest in the modern missionary movement of Christianity, which to him was part of the triumph of the Kingdom of God. All these strains of interest came together in his thinking, and led him to interpret Christian faith as " the faith that rebels " against all evils, material as well as spiritual, and that lays hold of the power of God which is able to give us the victory.

The student of theology may profitably trace this stream of thought from its sources and tributaries to its later reaches in the theology of our time. Thirty or forty years ago Cairns sometimes seemed to himself to be pursuing a somewhat lonely course in theology. But there were certain allies, known and unknown. There was a kinship, and a mutual influence, between Cairns's work and that of his friend Dr. A. G. Hogg, of Madras Christian College, author of *Christ's Message of the Kingdom* and *Redemption from this World*. An affinity has also been noticed with Bishop Gustav Aulén's interpretation of the original Christian message as a message about God's victorious battle in Christ against the elemental powers of evil, though there was no direct influence in this case. Still more striking is the parallel between Cairns's thought in *The Faith that Rebels* and a certain strain in the quite independent thought of Professor Karl Heim of Tübingen. Any student who is interested in such matters would find it highly profitable to read, alongside this volume, the chapter on miracles in Heim's recently translated work, *The Transformation of the Scientific World-View.*[1] He may also find an important tributary if he notes that Cairns, Hogg and Heim all acknowledge a debt to the work of a German theologian of a generation ago, Arthur Titius. And all of this is part of the broad and growing stream of thought which in our time is endeavouring to transcend the too narrowly " spiritual " conception of salvation, and to recover the New Testament conception of a total salvation of " spirit, soul and body," and indeed of cosmic redemption. In that whole story, which has now unrolled itself much further, and which still has many unanswered questions, Cairns's book, even if we find in it many things that we should wish to query, has an important place of its own.

Moreover, apart from the theological student's interest in research into movements of thought, this is the kind of book that it is good for us to read. It has a rugged beauty and eloquence, and it has a tonic quality which makes for faith because it is so " full of faith " itself. I hope this new edition may give it a fresh lease of life and make it familiar to a new generation.

March 1954 DONALD BAILLIE

[1] SCM Press London, Harper New York, 1953. *Cf.* also a much earlier essay on " Supernatural Healing " in Heim's *The New Divine Order*, SCM Press, 1930.

PREFACE TO THE FIFTH EDITION

In the Preface to previous editions of this book I have expressed my obligation to the Trustees of Auburn Theological Seminary, under whose auspices the Russell Lectures on which it was based were delivered, and to the friends who have aided me in its preparation or have helped me to clear my own thoughts on its subject.

In this Preface I should like to make my grateful acknowledgments to those who have reviewed it, and to those who have corresponded with me about it. I had no expectation when it was written, that it would meet with so friendly a reception. It has been made quite clear to me since then that the dissatisfaction with the prevailing theories of the Gospel miracles to which the book gives expression was shared by a much larger number of people than I had supposed, and that the mind of the Church is open on the whole subject in a way that it was not twenty years ago.

It has been interesting to note, also, that among all the many suggestions and criticisms, public and private that have reached the writer not one has questioned the exegetical part of the argument. They have been one and all directed either to the constructive or practical parts of the book. Some of them seem to me to be very much to the point. I make no claim to have completely explored or satisfied myself about the whole range of the argument, and the pressure of daily work has compelled me to abstain from applying the central idea of the book, the power of Faith over the outward as well as the inward world, to the difficult and as yet not completely solved problem of the real meaning of our Lord's apocalyptic teaching. I have never felt that the book was more than in the strict sense an essay, with the solution carried as far as at the moment I was able to carry it, and stated at the moment in the hope that others might be able to carry it further. I hope to have made it reasonably clear that neither of the two existing theories, the Traditional or the Modernist, can really be reconciled with the substance of the teaching of Jesus, as it is recorded in the Synoptic Gospels, and I have seen no reason since the book was published to depart from any of its essential positions.

The trained philosopher will expect a much fuller handling of the ultimate questions of Theism than he will find explicitly discussed in this volume. There is no full discussion there of the relations between nature and personality, the natural and the supernatural, and the limitation of natural selection as applied to the moral convictions of man, or the hard problem of pain in the animal world, though I hope he may discern an underlying scheme of thought, coherent with itself, though as yet at certain points tentative. I have abstained from dealing more fully with these questions in part from a fear of overloading and obscuring the argument, and have confined myself as far as possible to the immediate difficulties in believing in the miracles of Jesus felt by the thoughtful modern student. The underlying issues can only, I think, be clearly and adequately discussed in their full context in the philosophy of religion. To some of these I hope to return later in another volume. Objection has also been taken to the absence of any detailed use of criticism of the Gospel narratives. If it could be shown that the accepted results of that criticism made any material difference to the general argument there would be real force in this objection. But so far as my own limited knowledge goes, the characteristic idea, the power of faith over nature, is present in all the sources. It seemed therefore at this point also unnecessary to load the argument with unnecessary material.

It is clear that the difficulty most commonly felt is that involved in the nature miracles, the Feeding of the Four and Five Thousand, the Walking on the Water and the Stilling of the Storm. Personally, I see no adequate reason to question the substantial historicity of these narratives. It is, of course always possible that details may unconsciously have been exaggerated, narratives duplicated and so forth. The general argument does not imply at any point the inerrancy of the narratives, or as a critic, Professor Raven has said "an uncritical acceptance of all miracles on the sole ground that Jesus is unique and could do anything and everything."[1] I am afraid this is a hasty impression rather than one that has really grasped the whole argument. But I regret to have given so friendly a critic any reason for such a hasty impression. As a matter of fact I think that the narrative of the finding of the stater in the mouth of the fish is probably an unconsciously heightened narrative and that that of the blasting of the fig tree is probably a parable misunderstood by later reports as a miracle.

But I very definitely object to the exclusion of any really significant sign on the sole ground that it is too remarkable to be credible. I think there is perhaps a similar haste in the following statement that the book

[1] *Jesus and the Gospel of Love*, p. 252.

"identifies evil with suffering." I desire to speak very humbly about the great mystery of suffering. It may be that as yet "we have no sounding line for those vast depths." But I would draw a deep distinction between moral and physical evil, in as much as the former is unconditionally evil. No sin ought ever to have been. We cannot say the same of all physical evil. Where there are criminals, there ought to be prisons, and penalties. Yet the better a society becomes the more prison and penalties will go. They are obviously evils though relative evils. It is in this category of relative evils that I would put human suffering generally. As a matter of fact this judgment of it is common to practically the whole human race and finds expression in the Christian conception of heaven as the place where "God shall wipe away all tears from all eyes."[1] The miracles I take to be fragments of heaven, parts of the new divine order appearing in this present world, emergent islets of a new continent that is appearing above the waters, in response like the first creation to the "brooding Spirit" of God.

It is undoubtedly true that suffering can become the means of the highest good, and that faith can therefore even "rejoice in tribulation." But I think we are leaving both Biblical ground, and the ground of ordinary common sense, if we refuse to look on suffering generally as a real though relative evil. I cannot think that Jesus Christ did. Harnack may have put the matter one-sidedly, yet

[1] Professor Strachan's objection to the passage (p. 151) in the book in which it is said that "the positive evils which man endures from the great system of Nature are contingent . . . and are not part of the Eternal order at all," would seem to imply the eternity of suffering even in heaven. (Vide *The Authority of Christian Experience*, p. 69).

I cannot but think in the main truly, and was it seems to me on sure historical ground, when he wrote: "To him all evil, all misery, is something terrible; it is part of the great realm of Satan; yet he feels the power of the Saviour within him, and he knows that all progress is possible only by over-coming weakness and disease."[1] I am not quite clear, however, in what respect Professor Raven would differ from this summary and the general position of this book, and therefore further discussion of his criticism would be unprofitable.

On the nature miracles in general I would say that it would be unfortunate if any one should be put off the main line of the argument of the book by any difficulty he may feel about their complete historicity. Its main theme is to discover the true interpretation of what our Lord said about Faith and the ideal range of its powers. It is an endeavour to re-open this question and to focus upon it the attention of Biblical scholars and of theologians more competent than myself. If our Lord's teaching about Love is of vital importance for our whole understanding and treatment of man, his teaching about Faith must surely be of like moment for the understanding of the nature and the ways of God. This is, indeed, the central interest of Theism. From the point of view of this book these nature miracles are of religious value because they illustrate and enforce that teaching. They are the kind of deeds one would expect of the "Author and Perfecter of Faith," if all that he said about Faith were true.

But I can understand the position of a man, who on critical or historical grounds finds the evidence for them insufficient. Rejection of the narratives merely on these

[1] *What is Christianity?* pp. 57, 58. (Crown Theological Series.)

grounds would not seriously affect the general argument so long as the general principle of the ideal power of Faith over apparently adverse eternal nature is admitted. It is only when the nature miracles are ruled out as impossible or ethically unsound, that the issue becomes one of vital importance to the argument.

More than one friend has raised the point as to whether the whole conception of the miracles of our Lord contained in the book does not undermine the principle of order in nature on whose constancy the whole social and moral life of man depends. This, of course, raises the whole issue between the scientific and the religious interpretation of nature and of human life. I hope to deal with this perennial subject also more fully in a volume to which I have referred. I would only say here that I do not believe that, even if the human spirit rose to a far greater range of control over nature by virtue of spiritual development far beyond anything that is now on the horizon, any such irrational chaos would come into being as is supposed. The view of the book is that all such control is in the last resort Divine control. It is wrought by the Spirit of God in answer to the prayer of faith and hope and love. If this were carried to its perfection in the Kingdom of God we should have, I believe, not a chaos but a new order of a freer and larger kind, a transformation of the existing natural order, but still a manifestation of the Divine Reason and Love.

Mr. Weatherhead in a recent attractive and original volume[1] gives forcible expression to a view of the miracles of our Lord, for which he appeals to the authority of Augustine and which I remember to have been expressed in conversation by my old teacher Professor Herrmann.

[1]*His Life and Ours*. (Hodder and Stoughton.)

"A miracle," said the latter, "if it happens, is simply an unclassified phenomenon. You see a will-o'-the-wisp light and you cannot explain it in terms of your ordinary knowledge and so you call it a miracle. But as your knowledge extends and you come to know more about the atmosphere and the gases exhaled by marsh land you are able to bring it under law and it ceases to be a miracle." That there is truth in this view I should not question. All God's ways with man must surely be reasonable ways in the highest sense of reason. But they need not be mathematically calculable ways! Experience leads one to distrust the men who make diagrams of human history and numerical calculations of the hours and weeks when "Days of the Lord" will come. Nor will it, I think, ever be possible to make an exact science of human history, though that a looser and freer order prevails there than in Nature I am sure. So I question if miracles will ever be made matters of natural law. As I view them they belong rather to the domain of freedom, human and Divine. What the place of Nature will be in the Kingdom of God, no man can tell. It may be as unlike the present as a block of marble to a finished statue. There will be order and beauty in it even though it be a very different order from the apparently rigid uniformities of the cosmos as we know it today. Out of the merely physical order, there has arisen the order of biology and out of the biological order has come the freer and yet, in the real sense, ordered world of human history. Seen from the stage immediately below it each new advance into freedom might well have seemed a step into anarchy. Why should there not be a higher world still, which like each of these earlier stages has its roots in the more rigid domain beneath, and yet has its branches in a freer and higher zone? But both question and answer are perhaps too speculative to be urgent.

Another question raised has been as to the view of the personality of Christ which underlies the general view of the book. Does it regard him as simply a man filled by the Holy Spirit of God, or as "God manifest in the flesh" in the full apostolic sense of the words? Again, I would say that I have been unwilling to load the argument with too much theology, and have in the main contented myself with endeavouring to bring out quite plainly the teaching of the Gospels that the "signs" are works of the "Spirit" and not of the inherent divinity of the Son. The latter view seems to me to be simply a gloss invented by later theology without any encouragement from the New Testament itself. But the entire background of my own thought is that there was a real, a new and a unique coming of God to man in Jesus Christ, a true Incarnation.

INTRODUCTION

The discussion of the problem of the miracles of Jesus seems at present to have reached a kind of stalemate. For a long time past they have been regarded by the Christian Church as essentially evidential portents which were external signs, and had little or no meaning in themselves for the Christian view of God and the world. They belonged to the sphere of apologetics rather than that of theology. They have been looked at from this point of view alone alike by those who accepted and those who rejected them.

The former have defended them as bulwarks of the faith, rather than as part of the faith itself; and those who have abandoned them have done so merely because they were the point at which the scientific and religious views of the world seemed to come into sharpest collision. In order to ease the strain therefore, believing that these miracles were to-day of little direct religious value, they have abandoned them. The intellectual duel has been well maintained by the older school. For those who believe in a living personal God and in human freedom there is really very little of an intellectual case against the miracles of Jesus. But on the other hand the old argument from miracles has no longer the same central position in the Christian apologetics as it used to have. The centre of the argument for Theism and for Christianity to-day has moved into a new region from that of external proofs. and these are, even by their supporters, now regarded as being only of contributory value. Most modern religious thinkers base the case for Theism solidly on moral values and imperatives, and for Christianity upon the spiritual personality of Jesus. So for a long time past little that is really new has been said on either side, and almost nothing by younger writers. The most interesting recent book on the subject is curiously symptomatic of the general state of the question. In the earlier part of this volume[1] Dr Tennant in a few incisive chapters demolishes the philosophical argument against miracles, but in the concluding part expresses the opinion that, vitally important in earlier days as miracles were as evidence to the first believers, they are of little value for our generation.

On the other hand Modernism has contributed little that is new or important to the negative case. The only important new material that has been adduced by this school has been the knowledge of sub-conscious phenomena which has been gained during the last fifty years. The endeavour has been made to show that the narratives of our Lord's healing miracles can be best explained as mythical exaggerations of the phenomena of psycho-therapeutics, and that the Resurrection has a new light thrown upon it by what we know of phantasms of the living and the dead. I hope to show later

[1] *Miracle and its Philosophical Presuppositions* (London University Lectures, 1924).

that this new knowledge which we have is capable of quite another interpretation.

I cannot think that this stalemate is likely to endure. It seems to me that much deeper interests are involved in the whole question than are at present finding expression, and that the courses of thought are tending in such a direction as will open the whole subject afresh from new points of view.

This volume is an essay towards this end. I have been unable to find solid intellectual standing-ground in either the Traditional or the Modernist position. The former ignores the fact that Jesus Christ is uniformly represented in the Gospels as having a view of His own signs materially different from the view which the Traditional theory defends; the weak point of the latter is, first, that it also ignores the full force of this teaching, and that it tacitly admits certain *a priori* conceptions, which, if consistently carried through, would disintegrate those elements of Christianity which it retains.

Finally, the unconscious suppression of our Lord's own view by both alike seems to me to have serious consequences for the fundamental Christian ideas of God and the world, and also of the range and scope of ideal prayer.

I am well aware that the view which is set forth here has its own difficulties, and its half-solved and unsolved problems. The book is an exploratory essay rather than a dogmatic solution. I shall be content if I am successful in raising and stating the problem, and in inciting others to carry the solution further than I have been able to do.

The plan of the argument is as follows. I have endeavoured to set forth in some detail the two existing theories of the miracles of Jesus, which I have called the Traditional and Modernist views respectively, to explain them historically, and to indicate in detail their defects. I have then endeavoured to set forth the Old Testament and Jewish groundwork of thought which is universally presupposed in the Synoptic Gospels, without which we cannot possibly understand the significance which these signs had for those in whose presence they were wrought. I have then endeavoured to set forth in detail the uniform view of these signs which was taken by Christ and His contemporaries.

I have then discussed whether this view is wholeheartedly believable by modern men, and finally have in brief outline set forth what seems to me to be the necessary reaction of this view on the doctrines of God, of the world, and man, and its bearing on the solution of the problem of the tragic element in human experience.

I may add, as a personal explanation, that the book owes its origin to the fact that many years ago study of the Synoptic Gospels led me to see that there was more in the teaching of Jesus on the power of faith and the range of prayer than were finding expression in our current Christian thought and practice.

Fuller study, both of the Bible and of theology, has only confirmed and extended this view, and the pressure of the problem of the world due to the war has caused me to pursue the inquiry as to the changes in our outlook, both as regards thought and action, which would result from our taking this teaching of Jesus and carrying it logically through. The core of the whole book, therefore, is the exegetical section. We have here a clear issue. Does the interpretation which I have endeavoured to set forth give the natural meaning of His words ? Did He ever say anything in contradiction of that meaning ? Can His words fairly mean anything else ? I do not see that they can. I believe, further, that recent developments, both in philosophy and psychology, have almost unawares been effecting great changes in the whole climate of thought, which have rendered both the Traditional and the Modernist views of these "signs" of Jesus obsolete, and that the course of religious thought is sooner or later bound to bring up the whole question again in a new form. The subject therefore demands re-examination by Christian thought from every available point of view. Even a mistaken or defective theory, if rooted in serious thought, must in the end advance the ultimate solution. The main motive of this volume has been the desire to give the words of Jesus about faith their full meaning, and to seek to throw the light of that meaning on the central problem of theism and the mystery of human life.

CHAPTER I

THE RIVAL THEORIES OF MIRACLE —TRADITIONAL AND MODERNIST

THE history of miracles in the Christian Church has been strangely chequered. At first they were regarded as glories of the Christian faith. Nothing can be clearer from the earliest records than that the first generation of believers regarded them as creative and glorious deeds of the Divine Spirit —fragments of heaven and intimations of immortality. They were expressions on the human side of the very genius of prayer, and verifications of the confidence of the Church that it was the "third race," the new Humanity. So might an Athenian regard the works of his sculptors and dramatists and historians; the age of Elizabeth, the achievements of its voyagers and the *Faerie Queene*; our own time, the victories of commerce and science.

Nothing too can be clearer than that Christ gloried in the great deeds of blessing that God wrought through Him and His disciples. When His disciples came back and told Him that "even the devils were subject to them," He "rejoiced in the Spirit and said to them, I beheld Satan as lightning fall from heaven." These healings of tortured minds and bodies were the opening victories in the great campaign against sin and sorrow which would end in the total destruction of Satan's kingdom. At the end of His ministry the Fourth Evangelist represents Him as saying of the coming raising of Lazarus, "Said I not unto thee, that if thou wouldst believe, thou shouldst see the glory of God?" Nothing can be more futile than the endeavours made to-day by well-meaning commentators of both the Traditionalist and Modernist schools to show that Jesus disliked working His signs. He refused utterly to work useless and spectacular signs such as were asked of Him, but gloried in healing the bodies of suffering men, and never shrank from this beloved mission, save when it threatened to interfere with His even diviner work of preaching the Gospel.

Jesus, in fact, seems to have felt towards physical and mental disease precisely as every good modern physician feels towards it. I shall have something to say about this later in Chapter II when we have the evidence more fully before us. Meantime it is enough to say that in this respect He does not differ from the ordinary medical standpoint, nor can we understand Him unless we appreciate this. He always assumes that disease is part of the kingdom of evil, and never once does He give the slightest sign to the contrary. Not only does He try to heal all who are brought to Him, but He sends His disciples forth with a general commission to heal indiscriminately. His unvarying assumption, where there are failures, is that there has not been enough faith either on the part of the healers or of the sick or their friends and neighbours. His underlying idea can only be that God is always on the side of health rather than of disease, and that where the latter triumphs, something is as it ought not to be. There is nothing to be gained by evading or turning down what is the plain meaning of the Synoptic narratives. It is impossible to make coherent sense of them on any other supposition. Surely, also, the discoveries of modern science regarding the true nature of at least the great majority of diseases make this the only rational view. We now know that at least the majority of diseases, if not the whole of them, are due to the existence of minute living creatures who prey upon the human body from within. Man's first great struggle for progress was a fight with wild beasts of prey, wolves, tigers, and lions. His struggle to-day with disease is a struggle with wild beasts also. The only difference is that of the dimensions of the ancient and modern beasts of prey. It would seem to follow inevitably that we can only look rationally upon physical disease as we look upon the devastations of the wild creatures of the jungle. Disease is just as little or as much part of the Divine order in the one case as the other. It is surely as impossible to regard the one as the direct Divine will for man as the other. Indirectly they may both be regarded as part of that objective order which, as we shall see, penalises our ignorance, our apathy and indolence and cowardice, and educates us in better ways. In this sense and in this sense alone are they both together the Divine will for men. But they are evils, none the less, against which all right-thinking men should wage wise and resolute war, by striking at the real roots of the trouble.

It is not therefore at all surprising that the early Church should have gloried in this particular kind of miracle, and should have set itself to imitate its Master in this, as in deeper respects.

Such "miracles" were regarded as works and manifestations of the Holy Spirit, proofs that God was with the infant Church in its great enterprise. It is impossible to read the twelfth chapter of First Corinthians with an open mind, and not to see that this is the underlying view of the charismata or "gifts" of the Spirit, which mark out the Church as a Divine institution. In a writing of another branch of the Christian Church than the Pauline, the Epistle of James, we have the same underlying ideal practice. "When any one is sick [note the universality of the expression], let him call for the elders of the church. They shall lay their hands on him, and anoint him. The prayer of faith shall save the sick, and his sins shall be forgiven him." The Jewish colour here is stronger than in the Pauline Epistle, but the drift of it is the same.

Harnack[1] says that this was the ordinary Christian method of healing disease, until well down in the third century, when it was abandoned for what by that time had no doubt proved the more immediately effective method of striking at disease from the physical side of the psycho-physical organism, which method came in from the Greek culture; and he says that it was part of that fusion of Christian faith with Gentile thought and practice

[1] *Medicinisches aus der ältesten kirchengeschichte.*

which led to the development of Catholicism. The practice of maintaining official exorcists, which persisted in the Church for centuries, was a rudimentary survival of this early practice of healing all diseases by prayer which we find exercised in the New Testament. The beautiful chapters on the subject in Harnack's *Expansion of Christianity* give a moving picture of the hopes and aspirations of the early Church on this whole matter.

It is plain that all this is in full continuity with the Synoptic account of His "miracles," and that the early Church believed itself called to carry on the same mission as Jesus Himself practised, and which He commissioned His first disciples to carry on in His Name.

Not only did the early Church believe itself commissioned so to do, but it had no doubt as to its own powers.[2] Whatever theory we may have as to the authenticity of the closing section of St Mark's Gospel: "These signs shall follow them that believe: In My Name shall they cast out demons; they shall speak with new tongues; they shall take up serpents; and if they drink any deadly thing, it shall in no wise hurt them; they shall lay hands on the sick, and they shall recover" (Mark xvi. 17, 18)—there can be no real question that these words express the belief and practice of the first Christian century.[3] Taken in connec-

[2] See Appendix A.

[3] So Prof. Allan Menzies, *The Earliest Gospel*, commentary *in loco*. The full passage is as follows: "This is the experience of the Early Church, which fully believed itself to possess these powers in Matt. x., Luke ix. 10. In Mark's charge (iii. 15,

tion with the Synoptic narrative generally, with the Pauline Epistles, and with the Epistle of James, and what has been preserved of the earliest literature of the Church, they seem to me to leave no reasonable doubt as to the matter.

How long this period of optimistic and courageous faith lasted, I am unable from my own knowledge to say precisely. Certainly it extended far beyond the period in which the bulk of the New Testament writings took form. Harnack, as we have seen, puts the abandonment of this method in the third century, and traces it to a deviation from primitive Christian orthodoxy and custom.

But gradually these and the other phenomena of the Spirit diminished: "It was in the primitive days of Christianity, during the first sixty years of its course, that their effects were most conspicuous, but they continued all through the second century, though in diminished volume. The Montanist movement certainly gave new life to the "Spirit," which had begun to wane; but after the opening of the third century, the phenomena dwindle rapidly, and instead of being the hallmark of the Church at large, or of every individual community, they become merely the equipment of a few favoured individuals. "The common life of the Church has now its priests, its altar, its sacraments, its holy book and rule of faith. But it no longer possesses 'the Spirit and power.' As the

vi. 7) much less is claimed, and the deficiency is here made good. On Tongues, see Acts ii. and 1 Cor. xiv. On Exorcism, see Acts xii. 17, 18, 19. On recovery from poison of serpents, Acts xxviii. 3-5; healing the sick, James v. 14."

proofs of 'the Spirit and of power' subsided after the beginning of the third century, the extraordinary moral tension also became relaxed, paving the way gradually for a morality which was adapted to a worldly life." [4]

From this time on, miracles of healing became more and more wonderful exceptions, being associated with personalities of outstanding force or reputed sanctity, or with certain places which have acquired, mainly through some saint or apparition, a peculiar reputation for healing power. It was, of course, quite inevitable under these circumstances that they should change in character, and instead of being regarded as part of the normal manifestation of the Father's love, should instead become evidential portents, extraordinary proofs of His Divine favour for certain saints, and evidences of the Divine function of the Catholic Church. We pass by gradual transition into the luxuriant wilderness of mediæval myth and legend.

Into this field it is unnecessary to travel. Up to this point miracles are still regarded as glories of the faith, and, in so far, the uniform view of the New Testament and the early age is maintained. But they are rather glories of God's power than glories of His universal love. They are the normal accompaniment of the lives of the saints, and are miracles both of judgment and of mercy designed to awaken and to increase faith. As yet the critical spirit was asleep, so there was little limit to credulity. To those who believed in the stupendous and constantly repeated miracle of the Mass, it

[4] Harnack's *Expansion of Christianity*.

was in no way improbable that the most extraordinary things should happen in the lives of the saints, or after their deaths in contact with their relics or at places associated with their presence. The mediæval mind had no difficulty about the credibility of miracles. Like the mind of the earlier ages, it believed, also, in miracles wrought by the powers of evil, as well as by the powers of good.

With the Reformation a change began, and a more critical temper began to show itself regarding ecclesiastical miracles. The Lutheran and Reformed theologians could not look with the same eyes as their opponents upon the immense multitude of miracles which were believed to have manifested Divine power through those who, the Reformers believed, were on the side of Antichrist. Therefore, where these did not ascribe them to monkish invention, so far as they took note of them at all, they tended to ascribe them to demonic agency.

Luther believed profoundly in the power of believing prayer. His own prayers were believed to have recovered Melanchthon from a mortal illness. He says boldly in one of his great treatises that if we had faith enough, there is no disease that we could not cure. Nor had the Reformation theologians any difficulty about the New Testament miracles, nor, so far as I know, about the miracles of the early Church. The modern period only begins with the dawn of Rationalism, the gradual rise of the scientific conception of nature, and the growth of the critical spirit.

This put the religion of the eighteenth century in an acute difficulty on the whole subject of the miracles of the New Testament, and has since been the main factor in causing that extraordinary revolution of feeling which has transformed them from being glories of the faith of all, to being burdens on the faith of many modern Christians.

We can best see the whole situation of the time mirrored in the works of its two most powerful writers, Gibbon and Hume. Hume's argument, briefly put, is that the only conceivable way in which miracles can be proved is by human testimony. But the course of nature is proved by all experience to be unvarying, whereas testimony is proved by experience to be very liable to error. Nature is therefore more to be trusted than testimony. Therefore miracles can never be proved. It is clear that the argument would prove a great deal more than what is reasonable. It is enough for our purpose that it would prove out of hand that the Jesus of history never existed, for He is historically just as unique as any of His works.

Gibbon's case, however, shows the very real difficulty in which Protestant orthodoxy was now placed. The official Anglican position was that the miracles of the New Testament age were historical, and were granted as portents evidential of the truths which it taught. They were continued for a time that the young Church might be well founded. Similar but fewer signs were granted to the fourth or fifth century, and were later withdrawn as being no longer necessary. Enough in all were granted to authenticate the Divine approval of the Fathers of the early centuries, the standard of Anglican orthodoxy. By this convenient method the Roman conceptions were condemned and the Anglican standards maintained. So flagrantly dogmatic a construction of history failed to hold the youthful Gibbon's mind, which was aroused from its dogmatic slumber by Middleton's attack upon the veracity of the ecclesiastical miracles. Unwilling to leave the Christian faith and yet compelled to see that even the Fathers of the fourth or fifth century were sacerdotalist, he was driven to join the Church of Rome. But as his mind expanded and the spirit of his age entered into him, he found the Roman position untenable, and in the counter-recoil abandoned miracles altogether.

Now, apart altogether from the spirit of the age of Rationalism, and apart altogether from the fact that neither Gibbon nor Hume was temperamentally a religious man or had any desire to find God in history, it is clear that a great transformation had come over the whole idea of miracle since the early Christian age. The orthodoxy of the day was generating a view of it which is not really the view of the Synoptic Gospels, nor that of Jesus Himself. The view which Gibbon and Hume were rejecting is one which has only secondary interest for the modern Christian. The mediæval Church had spoiled the conception, but it was centuries before the Protestant Church realised the fact.

We have now in our review of the history reached the present-day situation. To-day we may say broadly that two conceptions struggle for the mastery—the Traditional and Modernist. I shall endeavour to state them both in their clearest form, though there are intermediate positions.

The Traditional view is in principle substantially the same as that taught by the Scholastic theologians of Roman Catholicism and Protestantism. The miracles of Jesus are true narratives of historical events. Their purpose was evidential; they were meant to give convincing evidence that God was on the side of Christ. Many traditionalists would put them more simply still, and would say that they are direct expressions of our Lord's Divinity, acts of creative power that could only be wrought by a Divine Being. They are, in any case, meant to authenticate His teaching and mission as Divine. They are not parts of the message, but proofs of its truth. They are seals attached to the document, not parts of the document. They are the crier ringing his bell to call attention to his message. The essential thing here is that they should be signs of Divine Power. Only this can make them unmistakably Divine. So was it with the miracles of Jesus, and above all, with His Resurrection. The crier rang His bell so hard that the contemporaries could not choose but hear. So was it also with the miracles wrought by the disciples. These were, one and all, evidential in character. Standing as the disciples did for Jesus Christ, power was graciously granted them by the Almighty to meet the exceptional circumstances, and to support them as they faced their mighty task of overcoming the world. It is assumed that it was revealed to them at the time the miracle was wrought, that God was willing to endue them with this exceptional power for the moment and the occasion. The whole reasoning turns on the idea that the miracles were exceptional, and that they were convincing portents. They were thus phenomena quite distinct from Divine providences or ordinary Divine answers to prayer, which were meant to be normal experiences in the life of the Christian. A distinction commonly drawn by the maintainers of this view was that, while in His Providence and in hearing prayer God worked through nature, in working miracles He, as it were, interfered with the course of nature, or "suspended" it.

Did miracles continue into early Christian times, and if so, when did they cease? Here Traditionalists are divided, not so much by reason of historical evidence as by virtue of the general religious view of authority which they hold. The orthodox Roman Catholic holds that these miracles have never ceased, but have been granted all the way down through history, and happen still, as, for example, at Lourdes, and the Holy Houses of Einsiedeln and Loreto. The Anglican position is not so definite or uniform. I have been unable, except in the case of Newman and Ward, to find that the Tractarians dealt much with the Patristic miracles. Many Anglo-Catholics to-day believe in the general continuity of the miraculous. In general, Anglican opinion is coloured on the one hand by respect for the testimony of the Fathers, and on the other by a general distrust of Mediævalism. Protestant Evangelical Christianity in the main would put the terminal period about the close of the New Testament age. In the case of the latter schools of belief, the cessation of miracles is ascribed to the disappearance of the need for such exceptional manifestations of the Divine Power. The underlying idea of this, historically, was that such exceptional manifestations were dangerous. The quaint phrase in use among those who first developed the traditional Protestant view, was that God made a " sparing use " of miraculous powers. I have no doubt that, as so often happened in theology, the political ideas in vogue in England during the period coloured the religious thought. The universe was regarded as a kind of British Constitution in which the normal government was carried on by the Reign of Law. When the Constitution got deadlocked, the sovereign intervened. But while this was provided for under the sanction of emergency, it was his wisdom to intervene as briefly and as sparingly as possible, and as soon as possible retire to his normal position as a " limited monarch."

I have endeavoured as fairly as possible, then, to outline the Traditional position. It has its strong points. It seems to conserve a due respect for the formidable uniformity of nature along with a recognition of the reality of miracle, and the possibility of a living Providence and the reality and power of prayer. It seems a safe mediating position, which does not put too great a strain upon belief on the one hand or on scientific necessities on the other, and it has all the advantage of being already in possession of the mind of the Church. Yet I do not think it can really bear close examination in the full light of present-day thought. It is too artificial, too obviously a compromise framed to avoid certain controversial extremes. It does not arise naturally out of the Gospel narratives, or out of the scientific necessities, but out of the historical situation in the century in which it originated. The weakness of it to-day is that that situation has changed. Science has filled up the many gaps in its own construction of the physical world, and is throwing out saps and parallels into the sphere of the psychical, and historical study of the New Testament period has greatly developed. The ideas which underlie its literature are much more fully understood. The traditional view of our Lord's miracles might, and no doubt did, satisfy the religious consciousness of scientific men of its own time, but that it does not so satisfy many of them to-day the growth of Modernism demonstrates.

But what, it may be asked, are the main difficulties of the Traditional view? (1) The first of these, I think, is that it does not really correspond to the New Testament idea of the miracles at all. It is a meaning imposed upon the New Testament by a supposed apologetic necessity. It is thus read into the Gospels rather than out of them. I shall endeavour to show this in detail in a subsequent chapter. Meantime, it may be enough to point out that the picture of Jesus as one who works Divine wonders for the purpose of calling attention to His message is strangely out of harmony with the Synoptic pictures. Over and over again in these narratives He refuses to work just such signs as the Traditionalist theory declares the miracles to have been, and condemns the spirit which demanded them as that of "an evil and adulterous generation." The latter adjective is taken from the Prophets, and means a generation in its heart alienated from spirituality and God. Spiritual truth is spiritually discerned by the childlike heart, not forced home upon dazzled senses and stunned minds by the blows of supernatural power. The story of the Temptation turns precisely upon this distinction between portents of power and signs of God's love and mercy, which by their own beauty attract "a free man's worship" as worthy of the Supreme.

The conception of Christ as a heavenly bellman is grotesquely out of keeping with Him of whom it was said, "He shall not strive nor cry, neither shall His voice be heard in the streets," a prophecy which is applied to Him by St Matthew. He is no herald with his tabard and trumpet, blaring and declaiming his monarch's commands, but a Son revealing His Father's ideal and heart towards the wandering children of men. "A true poet," it has been truly said, "does not write his poems in order to show that he is a poet. If he does he shows by so much that he is the less of a poet. He writes them because he cannot help it." So Jesus works His miracles because He cannot help working them, out of the sheer creative faith and hope and love within Him, which bring God in His healing power and man in his suffering and sorrow together.

(2) In some respects even more serious is the way in which the Traditional theory blunts the most remarkable feature of the Synoptic narratives, their steady reiteration of the close and vital relation between the works which Christ wrought and "faith." How large a part this plays in the Synoptic narratives will appear in the following chapters. The main object of this volume is to call

attention to this feature of the New Testament stories. That it is even yet so imperfectly recognised is due, I think, largely to the fact that the Traditional theory, in the light of which these stories are read, can get along quite well without laying any emphasis upon faith as the condition of the signs. Indeed, to some extent the view that the miracles are essentially manifestations of power so great that it must be Divine, is uncongenial to this insistence on this simple human condition, the absence of which is able apparently to set bounds to the manifestation of the power of God.

(3) Most of all must this be the case with reference to that form of the Traditional theory which ascribed the miracles of Jesus not to His perfect manhood, which makes it possible for the Spirit of God to work through Him, but to His essential Godhead resuming as it were its Divine power and acting, as is the Divine way, creatively in the world of space and time. Against this form of the Traditional theory we have not only the constant emphasis upon faith of which I have spoken, but the final and fatal fact that He transmitted His unique powers to mere men; and that St Paul had manifestly a totally different conception, which is expressed in his doctrine of the Spirit, and the charismata of the Church; and that finally it is quite without support from the texts themselves.

(4) The moment we begin to think out the Traditional view, and to account for the cessation of the miraculous gift, we come into insuperable difficulties. No matter what date we choose for

that momentous cessation, whether we put it about the fifth century, or at the close of the New Testament Canon, or within the lifetime of the Apostolic generation, the difficulty is the same.

The root idea is always that miracles are dangerous, a kind of heavenly explosive that may wreck the safe established order! Anything more grotesquely unlike the Apostolic outlook it would be difficult to imagine. It is eighteenth-century English Whig Constitutionalism, not the spirit of the Judean and Galilean dawn!

The explanation given is that the task of the early Church was so momentous and so difficult and perilous as to demand special aid from God. Hence these sporadic outbursts of Divine power were granted, for a comparatively brief period, and then withdrawn. One may fairly say to supporters of the view that miracles ceased with the New Testament age, Was not the Church in the following centuries in even greater extremities in its fight with Gnosticism within and the destroying fury of the Empire without? To others we may say, Why should the third, the fourth, or the fifth century have been the terminus—why, for instance, were there no miracles to prevent the Church from going astray in the critical sixteenth century, when its unity was again broken? One may say to them all, Is not this theory of an unconditional Divine withdrawal of miraculous powers altogether too artificial? Let us remember that no warning of such Divine withdrawal was ever given. Up to this period of privation, of reduction to an order less rich in Divine manifestation, it was regarded as high virtue and faith to hope for and to attempt such Divine signs. To hope for it after this period was to ask too much, to be out of touch with the new and more straitened reality, and yet no warning was ever given. Men were left to find it out by heartbreaking and faith-shattering failures.

The truth is, that here the Traditional theory will not fit the realities. Surely Harnack has given us a simpler and more satisfying solution in the passage quoted in last chapter. The miracles of the Spirit did not cease because of an unconditional Divine fiat; "The gifts and callings of God are without repentance." The miracles of the Spirit gradually ceased, because by compromise with the world the Church got out of touch with the pure grace of God. It no longer possessed the strong, unconventional faith of the first generation.

(5) Finally, the course of history has shown since these days, that wherever great spiritual personalities endowed with primitive energy of faith have arisen, faith has still been able to move mountains in the world of circumstances as well as in the world of the Spirit. The cumulative force of these considerations seems to me overwhelming.

I submit that the Traditional theory needs reconsideration. I recognise to the full its merits and achievements. It has maintained the essential thing, faith in the historical character of the facts recorded in the Gospels, but it has, it appears to me, done so at too great a cost, and has to-day been felt by very many unsatisfactory, even for the apologetic purpose for which it was framed.

So, throughout Christendom, there has arisen a new theory, which dates from the nineteenth century, the theory of Modernism.

The Modernist Theory

What in its outlines does this theory maintain? It originated in dissatisfaction with the Traditionalist theory. What was the ground of its dissatisfaction? It is not possible, within the limits of a brief sketch such as this, to go into all these reasons. To do so would carry us far into its antecedents in the great Rationalist movement of the eighteenth century. But there is no doubt that in our day the Modernist criticism of miracle is mainly due to its apparent conflict with physical science. Science has definitely established itself within the commonwealth of human knowledge. The technique of modern industry and commerce rests upon it, and so do the healing and other practical arts. On the other hand, deeply religious men, as many of the great Modernists have been, know well the vital importance to the soul of humanity of the great Christian ideals and faith. They believe that any conflict between science and religion must needs be a supreme disaster. This attitude to miracles is part of a projected concordat between science and religion. What in its essence is that concordat? The originators of the Modernist concordat believed that science had its true domain in the physical world, the world that was capable of being weighed and measured; and that within this dominion science had one universal principle of interpretation, the reign of law, or as it was otherwise called, the uniformity of nature. Translated into other terms, this means that the presupposition of all physical science is that nature is one closed system of universal causation. Science is the search for causes and for laws of their operation, the endeavour to show in detail that everything is "governed by law."

Now on this view the miracles of the New Testament must needs be regarded as anomalies. The Traditional theory regarded them as simply acts of God. It was essential to this view that the miracles should be inexplicable in terms of ordinary causation. Inasmuch as the causal system failed to account for them, they must be traceable to the Author and Lord of nature. Here there appeared to be a clean breach between the legitimate demand of science, its fundamental principle that nature was a uniform system, and the indispensable requirement of the Traditional theory that the physical causal system should be overruled, that Jesus should heal the sick, raise the dead, walk on the waves, and still the storm. The conflict between what was believed to be virtually an axiom of science and the very core of the Traditional theory of evidential portent appeared to be definite and absolute, and the framers of the Modernist concordat addressed themselves to the solution of the problem. They asked, first of all, was it really worth while for Christianity to stand by these physical miracles? They accepted, like the Traditionalists, the view that the miracles of Jesus had value only as evidential portents of Divine power. But, plainly, if this were so, the growing prestige of science, with its dogma of the uniformity of nature, was continually depriving them of that evidential power. They might still be held as pious opinions by believers, but they were of little use for the convincing of doubters touched by the scientific spirit. The fundamental question was raised as to whether it was really a spiritual and good thing to coerce faith by logical argument. Did not this make religious certainty a thing for the wise and prudent rather than for the childlike spirit? Spiritual truth, it was argued, must be spiritually discerned. Did not Jesus Himself teach this? The sayings which Jesus applied to the kind of signs desired by Scribes and Pharisees were applied to all His miracles, and so the picture of Jesus as one who disliked working "signs and wonders" then came into being, and was forced into the interpretation of the Gospels, in a most dogmatic and unhistoric way. The Traditional theory had already made the too obvious distinction between ordinary answers to petitionary prayer and miracle, and the Modernist theorists continued that unfortunate distinction, and suppressed the obvious fact that Jesus believed that prayer could alter the course of physical nature, and had inserted in His model prayer a petition for daily bread. They abandoned the physical signs wrought by Jesus as unhistorical, and, with these, the idea that prayer could in any way affect the outward course of nature. If such a practice were sanctioned in the New Testament, it could only be with the view of the petitioner gradually praying himself into submission to that divinely ordered course of nature. In the nature of the case its action could only be reflex action on the mind of the petitioner.[5]

What the Modernist view makes of Christ's conception of the Fatherly providence of God—"Be not anxious for the morrow, your heavenly Father knoweth you have need of these things," "the very hairs of your head are all numbered"—I do not know. I have never seen the question fairly faced. I do not see how it can possibly be harmonised with the general position that nature is a closed system, in virtue of which all miraculous happenings in the sphere of nature are excluded, and all prayer for external success is discouraged, or admitted only under impossible psychological conditions.

But while the whole physical environment of the human spirit is thus handed over to science and the unbroken causal laws, the Modernist theory stands firmly by the true autonomy of the inner life of man's spirit, and for the open road to God's personal intervention in the inner experiences of the soul. Eucken, for example, bases his whole philosophy on the new birth, Martineau maintains a real efficiency of the Divine Spirit within the psychical realm, and Harnack does the same.

It is part of the faith of Modernism that while no man has the right to expect God to come to his help in the world of outward circumstances, He can so help him by reinforcing all his inner moral energies as to enable him to triumph over

[5] For a striking example of this see F. W. Robertson's Sermon on *Prayer*, vol. iv. p. 23.

his trials and temptations, and so make the very outward ills themselves instruments of a higher good. In all these affirmations the Modernist view shows itself essentially Theistic and Christian; only in the theory of nature, which is involved in its rejection of all physical miracle, does it depart from the New Testament position. In many ways the Modernist school has done conspicuous service to the Christian cause in our modern world. Theism had no more powerful upholder in the difficult mid-Victorian time than Martineau, and to-day not a few of the ardent philosophical defenders of a spiritual view of life come from the Modernist camp. In the political and social life of the age there are no greater and more honoured representatives of the Christian values than some who have found their spiritual home in Liberal Christianity. The Modernist compromise has kept many troubled minds from making shipwreck of their faith, and can never be regarded by any one familiar with the life of our time and concerned with its main spiritual problems and issues, without sincere respect and gratitude. We live in an age of transition when, above all else, it is well to remember our Lord's words, "He that is not against you is for you"; and that on many of the greatest moral and spiritual issues the followers of Liberal Christianity have been in the very van of the fight, and sometimes beyond it, it is happily impossible for any one who knows the facts to deny.

But when one turns from the individuals to the intellectual system and asks whether the delimitation of frontiers which Modernism has supported is really tenable to-day, it is another matter. It is not really a frontier determined by the physical conditions but one which is dictated by the exhaustion of the combatants, and which, as soon as they have recovered their energies, they are bound to abandon. It is really impossible to cut the unity of the world into two clearly divided halves in this way, to assign the world of physical nature to the sway of the causal nexus, and the psychical and spiritual world to autonomy and the Divine Spirit. Neither religion nor science can long consent to a truce so hollow, indeed it has long been visibly breaking up before our eyes.

Science has gained greatly in boldness since the Modernist concordat first took form, and has extended its methods into the realm of psychophysics and psychology proper. We are at the moment face to face with the new determinism of modern psychology both in the Behaviourist theories and in Freudian psycho-therapeutics. To warn it off from this territory and repel it to the Victorian limits is impossible. On the other hand, can religion and ethics really rest content with that conception of physical nature as a closed and uniform system which is really at the very heart of the Modernist concordat?

I shall have to examine this question in detail later. Meantime it is enough to say that, if logically carried through, the closed system idea of nature makes an end not only of miracle and the power of prayer to influence the ordinary course of events, but of human freedom, and any real individual guidance and providence of God in human affairs.

But holding discussion of this over meantime, I shall confine myself here to the question of whether the Modernist exclusion of physical miracles from the Gospels leaves the real picture of Jesus intact, or vitally modifies it and changes thereby the whole conception of God, and the whole colour of the Christian life.

We have here to face a notable modification which of late years has, almost without notice, taken place in Modernism. The older type rejected all the physical miracles indiscriminately. If we go back to the literature of the Tübingen school of New Testament criticism (and the famous *Leben Jesu* of Strauss), we find the healing miracles grouped with the rest, and wherever a narrative in the Gospels or the Acts contains such narratives, it is at once suspect, and the batteries of criticism are brought to bear upon it, as either mythical or legendary. In this the writers followed faithfully the spirit of the materialistic science of their day, which did not admit of the possibility of anything analogous to the New Testament miracles of healing in current experience. Of course this compelled a much more drastic handling of the text of the Gospels than is to-day necessary.

To-day the position is completely changed. We now know much about the reciprocal relations of mind and body, the singular phenomena of hypnotism, suggestion, faith-healing, and psychotherapeutics, which have brought these healing miracles of Jesus within range of our experience.

The simple truth is, that in spite of the rough distinction between organic and functional maladies which medical science still draws, and which an extension of the powers of the microscope any day may modify, we do not really know the limits of the ideal power of the mind over pathological conditions. Modernism has here partially followed the lead of science, and is now willing to accept many, if not all, of the healing miracles of Jesus. But again, it patiently accepts the limits which our present-day experience still sets. We have no real analogies to the walking on the waters and to the control of the storm, and we have certainly none to our Lord's Resurrection, and so applying the standards of our everyday experience and making them the limits of the credible, these narratives are treated precisely as those of the healing miracles were treated seventy years ago.

One question, however, it may be noted, is completely ignored. Is this undetermined influence of mind over body, which is now conceded, really capable of being harmonised with the closed system idea of physical nature? I fail altogether to see that it can. How can mind have real power over bodily tissue and energy within a closed physical system? We seem to have a direct contradiction in terms. But if the system of physical nature can be deflected by the mind of man, is it really coherent thinking to say that it is unscientific to believe that its course cannot be influenced by the Mind and Will of God?

But passing by this very pertinent point for the moment, and accepting the changed point of view of Modernism, does the clearing out of the nature miracles, and above all of the Resurrection of our Lord, from the sphere of the historical, leave the picture of Jesus in essentials just what it was before?

Let every one read these Synoptic Gospels anew —and let him get the full picture of Jesus as they present it fresh in his mind, in all His glorious war not only with the sins of men, but with the whole tragic element in human experience, suffering, sorrow, and death—His victories over the destroying powers of nature, plague, famine, and storm, culminating in His final victory over the grave—and he will understand the victorious energy of the first great Christian enterprise, the glow of confident optimism and power with which it adventured forth on its mission of carrying the Gospel to every creature, and swept on, overleaping the wellnigh impassable barrier of Jewish nationalism, from Jerusalem to Antioch, and from Antioch to Rome. If we can once overcome the instinctive difficulty about miracles of any kind, the whole story reads like a unity, it makes the impression of being real history, much more than the laborious Modernist reconstructions of it based on the idea that the empty grave was a mistake.

If Jesus actually wrought these victories not only over human sin but human tragedy, we can understand why the Apostles called Him "the Prince of Life," and why the first great real difficulty was not why He should have risen again, but why He ever came to be subject to death at all. For that this was their real problem, the least study of the Acts and the Pauline and Petrine Epistles must make plain. How are the truly astonishing vitality, hope, and power which Jesus communicated to His disciples explained in the Modernist lives of Jesus? Do they really account for the spirit of the first Christian generation?

We have had quite a number of these attempted biographies of Jesus all written on the assumption that the miracles of Jesus were quite immaterial to the historical figure, and could be omitted without injury to the substance of His message. These range through all the shades of Modernism, from Strauss and Renan on to Oscar Holtzmann, Frenssen, Middleton Murry, and other popular writers. The trouble with one and all of these is that the figure they present is really quite different from the figure in the Synoptic Gospels, as different as the rather feeble Jesus of most modern painters is from the transfigured Christ of Raphael. The figure in the Gospels is full of victorious energy and power over all the dark and tragic elements in life. He is "prince of life" and victor over death. When He submits to the cross and grave, it is out of His own freedom. But in the Modernist lives the tragic element in physical nature is regarded as irresistible and immovable by even the faith, love, and prayer of Jesus. So the death of Jesus becomes a physical fate rather than a freely chosen spiritual destiny. He goes as a victim to death, not as a conqueror giving His rights away. The ideal Christian temper then becomes a noble stoicism towards all outward ills, rather than a conquering optimism. How on this view Jesus is supposed to be able to heal disease, Modernism leaves entirely unexplained.

Let any one read the Gospels afresh, and see if their whole spirit is not one of conquering optimism. They record the greatest attack in all history on sin and death. It is only in this double context that we can really understand the story, or see the place in it of the miracles and the Resurrection. Not only unbelief, hatred, and despair, but disease, famine, storm, and death itself, go down before the Prince of Life. What though the story remains unfinished? It looks towards the final victory over all sin and all mortal tragedy, which is symbolised in apocalyptic language as the Return of the Lord.

Now, turn from these Gospels and read the same story as it appears under the Modernist necessity of excluding miracle. Such books often give us a moving and noble picture of Jesus of Nazareth, but the whole ethos has been subtly changed. He has broken out of the tyranny of sin, but, just like the rest of us, is subject to the full human entail of disease and death. His crucifixion is not a freely chosen destiny. It is a fate: and the whole story of the Resurrection is due to the fond illusions of the disciples, for which indeed we must hold Him partially responsible, because of the exaggerated estimation of Himself and His powers which He taught and encouraged. Indeed I can never read even the best Modernist accounts of what happened at the resurrection without feeling that the whole story is extraordinarily depressing. There hovers around it a neurotic element of ecstasy, hallucination, and over-belief, which enables us perhaps to acquit Him of full responsibility for the pathological condition into which His disciples came, but which inevitably suggests that in Jesus we had one who should rather have been taken care of than crucified. Master and disciples alike should have been under medical supervision. "Sacred moments," said Renan, "in which the passion of one possessed gave to the world a resuscitated God!"

In reading the Modernist accounts of the whole Resurrection period, we are moving in the atmosphere of a clinique, a bog of neurosis. This, of course, quite suits the general view of Materialism, but it goes ill with the Christiàn faith which inspires Modernism. And it suits very ill with the history, with the breadth, sanity, and insight of the Galilean mission and the magnificent vitality and power of the early Church, which, we all alike admit, was recreated by the faith in the Resurrection.

The many ingenuities of Modernist writers at this point betray their uneasiness. It is denied, for instance, that St Paul means anything more by the Resurrection of Jesus than that the Spirit of Jesus ascended to the Father. As if every orthodox Jew of the time did not believe in the survival and escape of the spirit at death; as if St Paul, like every orthodox Jew, did not believe that the death of the body resulted from sin! A mere spiritual escape of the spirit would never have satisfied his demand that the Redeemer should wholly have overcome death. As if, finally, the plain meaning of the whole Resurrection narrative in First Corinthians did not mean that Jesus rose again in the full sense that His body rose in transfigured form! The idea of Christophanies inspired by the risen Christ, the telegram theory of Keim, is almost as hopeless. It would mean that while Christ's body was still mouldering in the grave, He suggested to them that it was risen, and so created the historic error which Modernism repudiates.

Finally, we are left with the old difficulty. What became of the body of Jesus? We are told that no doubt somehow it was lost. Is it then so easy for a human body to get lost at any time? How it could get lost in the tempest of love and hate of the Jerusalem of that day, it passes the wit of man to determine. Was there no Antigone among all these women to stand by and remember the place of the body of the Lord? Is it likely that Mary was less loyal to her Son than the Greek maiden to her brother? Was there no Sadducee or Pharisee with sufficient foresight and vigilance to destroy the early faith at its birth by producing the body? Is that like what we know of Caiaphas?

We are told by not a few Modernists that their real difficulty with miracle is not any *a priori* obstacle, but the want of evidence. Surely that is not the case here, at least. The impression which the whole handling of the Resurrection story irresistibly brings home is that here, at least, the *a priori* difficulty is the all-determining inhibition.

I am far from thinking that it is not a legitimate factor in weighing up the sober history of the whole matter. But I submit that that difficulty of believing in the unprecedented should have been taken earlier. It is part of the faith of Modernist Christianity that Jesus is absolutely unprecedented.

The personality of Jesus destroys the *a priori* improbability. In the end it seems to me that the reasoning which demands that we shall reduce the resurrection faith to hallucinations of over-strained men and women, and the resurrection fact to an absolutely ordinary resolution of the body of Jesus to its physical elements, demands the reduction of the uniqueness of Jesus also. Clearly in the background, behind all these confused theories of the resurrection, there is something much more powerful than want of historical evidence at work.

There can surely be little doubt that, if one can believe in the fact of the Resurrection and the empty grave, it makes far better history of the whole story than any form of the vision theory. It makes sense and unity of all the events, it makes the disciples intelligible as human beings all through, instead of resolving them into psychical riddles; above all, it makes a unity of the figure of Jesus Christ and sense of the New Testament. Finally, as I hope to show later, it gives us a profound and illuminating revelation of the innermost nature of the Universe, instead of making the riddle of the painful earth still more difficult, as it unquestionably does, if the earthly story of Jesus ends with the Cross rather than with the Resurrection.[6]

For all these reasons the Modernist view seems to me even less tenable than the Traditional.

I hope to show later, in more detail than is possible at this stage of our argument, how seamed

[6] This is powerfully brought out in *The Mind of the Disciples* and *The Rising Tide of Faith*, by the Bishop of Pretoria.

with inner contradictions is the whole speculative position of Modernism; but enough has meanwhile been said, I trust, of the difficulties of both views to justify us in endeavouring to open some new path.

In seeking to discover this, it is necessary to go back to the Bible itself, and see if its teaching is rightly translated by either Traditionalist or Modernist.

I hope to be able to show that the idea of the miracles of Jesus which both hold in common, *i.e.* that they are primarily evidential portents, seals attached to the Divine message to authenticate it, is mistaken, and that they are instead part of the message itself; and that instead of this adding to their difficulty, it greatly lightens it, and enhances our whole conception of the worth of the Christian revelation. But the starting-point of the whole argument of this book is that it claims to present the Scriptural view. When all is said, the Gospels have a clear and coherent account of our Lord's teaching as regards the nature of His signs, which is neither that of Traditionalism nor Modernism. The next section of the book is thus an exegetical study. The closing section will endeavour to set this conclusion in the general context of modern thought and doctrine.

CHAPTER II

THE OLD TESTAMENT BACKGROUND

It is necessary at this point to define clearly the limits of this essay. It is not an endeavour to deal with the whole subject of the miracles recorded in the Bible. Much confusion has, I believe, resulted from the endeavour to frame a theory of the miraculous which might be sufficiently wide to include all the miracles of the Bible. Having inductively framed such a conception, the apologist comes with it to the Gospel narratives and imposes it upon them, taking them as instances of that which he has already defined. The result has been that not a few of the essential characteristics of the "mighty works" of Jesus have been obscured by this unfortunate method.

The method pursued in this essay is quite different. We shall begin with the Gospel narratives themselves. This course, I trust, will justify itself for two reasons. First of all, there is no comparison between the Old Testament miracles and the New in their vital importance for living faith to-day. It is of little moment for faith whether Elijah actually called down fire from heaven upon the sacrifice at Carmel, whereas it is of the utmost moment whether Jesus rose from the dead on the third day.

Secondly, I hope to show that the great majority of the Gospel miracles are associated with the teaching of Jesus about faith in a way which has no parallel in the records of most of the Old Testament miracles. They are also far more closely interwoven with the whole fabric of New Testament thought.

These reasons alone are sufficient to justify this limitation of scope, and to warrant us for the time at least in allowing the New Testament narratives to make their own impression upon us. The same reasons warrant us in setting aside from this part of our inquiry the whole traditional theory of miracle, whose rise and progress has already been noted. We shall try to start afresh from a return to the Synoptic Gospels, which speak simply of the signs, the works, and the wonders of Jesus. What we are concerned with is not whether Jesus wrought "miracles" in the sense in which Bishop Butler or Emerson, or apologists generally, have used the word, but whether He healed the sick, stilled the storm, and rose from the dead.

So much then being premised, we shall now endeavour to set forth the view of miracle contained in the Synoptic Gospels themselves.[1]

Now when we enter on this inquiry, we find that we cannot reach the heart of the matter without the Old Testament. But we do not use it as our fathers used it or as did those apologists who

[1] I am indebted in this review of the teaching of Jesus to my friend Prof. A. G. Hogg's *Message of the Kingdom*, which has confirmed and developed my own reading of the Gospels.

endeavoured to compress the miracles of Jesus into one mould with those of the Old Testament. We use it in order to understand the world of thought in which Jesus and His disciples lived and acted. "The Old Testament," said Ritschl in a pregnant sentence, "is the lexicon of the New." We need to know the Hebrew inheritance of thought alike in its earlier and in its Jewish developments, if we are really to understand the thoughts and words and deeds of Jesus. For it is quite clear that in the first instance He spoke to His own contemporaries, and that we can therefore only understand His real meaning if we first make ourselves familiar with those general conceptions of God and His ways with men which were part of the common good of the Jewish people, and which Jesus shared with them. This principle is now universally recognised among all scholars. Whenever we come therefore on any mysterious or half-understood idea of Jesus, we have to consult the lexicon of the Old Testament in its Jewish edition. We apply that principle without hesitation when we are examining the New Testament ideas of sacrifice, of law, of judgment, and so forth. For our present purpose then we must ask what were the Old Testament presuppositions which governed the thoughts of the Apostles as they noted and pondered over the great deeds of their Master. Unless we do this, we shall come to these deeds with our modern presuppositions only, and the inevitable result will be that we shall miss their true meaning.

The Old Testament ideas which are relevant

and essential here for the true understanding of the Gospel narratives of the great deeds of Jesus are four in number: (1) the ideas of the Divine Covenant and its human correlative Faith as the supreme virtue of the true Israelite; (2) of the Moral Order of the world; (3) of the Spirit of God; and (4) of the Kingdom of God.

I. The Covenant and Faith

The fundamental and inclusive idea of the religion of ancient Israel was that it was in Covenant with God. We have of late become again familiar with the word, which had almost become obsolete as applied to moral and religious questions, by the solemn institution of the Covenant of the League of Nations.[2] That Covenant, however, is a compact between nations. It is a bi-lateral Covenant in which the parties are on more or less equal terms. They undertake with each other to observe certain rules, and the arrangement is entered into for the common advantage. There is no "grace" in it. It was quite otherwise with Israel's Covenant. There could be no such equality between the High and Holy One and His destined people.

Such a Covenant can only begin by an act of pure and sovereign grace on His side. He must take the initiative and He must maintain it throughout His whole relation with His people. That He

[2] I take it that we have here the Old Testament conception, mediated through Calvin, mediated again through the Presbyterian, Woodrow Wilson, to whom we owe the main inspiration of the League.

has done this transcendent thing, and that He remains faithful and constant to His grace is the sustaining conviction of Hebrew religion. It underlies the whole piety, law, and sacrifice of the people, as it underlies their whole historic life and achievement. By His pure sovereign grace, God has called their forefathers, welded their tribes into a people, given them a law and a land, and promised to be to them all that God can be, in the way of loving them, caring for them, and training them. In the strength of that initiating saving act of God they undertake to be to Him a true and faithful people. Such is the Covenant, and the Covenant relationship within which the whole religious life of Israel moves.

In the nature of the case such a Covenant could only be instituted by a historic act of God, and it was to the Covenant given at Sinai that Israel looked back as the foundation of its life as a chosen and covenanted nation. But its histories carried back the idea to the earlier stages of its life, and the priestly writer in particular thinks of that preparatory period as of a succession of covenants, with Noah and the "world's grey fathers," with Abraham and Isaac and Jacob. But it was above all to the deliverance from Egypt and the Covenant made through Moses at Sinai, that the piety of Israel looked as revealing the covenant grace of God.

Now again in the very nature of the case, this whole conception of the Covenant determined Israel's highest conceptions of the soul of true religion.

What did God ask of His people? What were the human obligations involved in this transcendent grace? We get various levels of insight here in the consciousness of Israel. In general the prevailing idea is that Israel's obligations are summed up in the words "obedience" and "righteousness." The Covenant at Sinai was not with the individual but with the nation, and the ordinary Hebrew, when he thought of "righteousness," thought of it as "a right attitude towards the existing constitution and conduct in harmony with its traditions."[3] The "righteous man" is one who "occupies the right moral and religious standpoint, and carefully abstains from wickedly transgressing the great ordinance of human and Divine justice."[4]

We find this stage of piety reflected in those Psalms in which the writer appeals to his "righteousness" as the ground of his appeal to God. But the discipline of Israel's history drove its moral thought deeper. The conscience became more deeply awakened by the presence of calamity, and the finer mind of Israel came to put its whole confidence more and more in the pure grace of God. Along with this there went an ever-deepening emphasis on the necessity of faith as the supreme virtue. The one follows inevitably from the other. If salvation is only from the pure grace of God, then it can only realise itself through deepening and widening faith, faith in the God who initiates and maintains the Covenant, mani-

[3] Davidson, *Old Testament Theology*, p. 274.
[4] Schultz, *Old Testament Theology*, vol. ii. p. 23.

festing Himself in it, and in the history of those who trust Him wholly within that Covenant. "Here lies the essence of man's being right with God, his response by faith to His grace in accepting the Covenant, and the continued exhibition of this condition of mind in the man's life and conduct. The righteous acts for which he is found righteous are only the exhibition of his attitude towards God and His covenant of Grace. To be righteous is to be right, *i.e.* to be found taking towards God's Covenant, which is a thing having as its principle grace, the right attitude; and this attitude is faith." [5]

Schultz is equally emphatic as to this fundamental position of faith in Hebrew piety.[6] The Divine life communicated by grace can be received by faith alone. Hence in the Old Testament as in the New, faith is the subjective condition of salvation.

"To surrender himself wholly and unreservedly to the Redeemer of Israel as his God, to accept the salvation embodied in the Covenant as his salvation, to acknowledge and love the ordinances of life as revealed in it as the ordinances of redemption . . . all this is what makes a true Israelite. Without this faith there is no morality, since faith in this God, as the only God of Salvation, is the first commandment." "As faith is the cause of salvation, so unbelief is the cause of all Israel's misery. It allows his conviction to be determined by what is material, by the power of the world, external

[5] Davidson's *Old Testament Theology*, p. 279.
[6] *Op. cit.*, p. 31, vol. ii.

misfortune and a sense of his own strength; it is faint-hearted doubt as to the power of God, or haughty defiance of his will."[7] It has sometimes been said that there is comparatively little use of the word "faith" in the Old Testament. As compared with its constant repetition in the New Testament, that is true. But the idea itself under different names and grammatical forms is very frequently referred to. If we take it with its synonyms, "belief" and "trust," we shall find the call for faith pervading all the deeper experience and thought of the Psalmists and Prophets, and present, moreover, as the mainstay of all heroic character and life in the Old Covenant. Therefore never was there a truer account of the religion of Israel given than that in the eleventh chapter of the Epistle to the Hebrews. The writer had learned in the school of Jesus to understand the very soul of the religion of his people. The whole thought of the Old Testament turns round these two poles, the grace of God and the response of faith and fidelity on the part of man. Perfect goodness according to Old Testament religion, and this is true of the Jewish version also, is equivalent to perfect faith.

II. The Moral Order of the World

The second great principle of Old Testament religion which we must grasp if we are to understand the works of Jesus, is that there is a Moral Order of the world.

The supreme achievement of the Hebrew race

[7] Schultz, vol. i. p. 36.

in human history was its identification of the supreme Power over all things, in which all religions have believed, with the Power which manifested itself in the moral ideal. The genius of Israel finds its highest expression in the great saying of Jeremiah, "Let not the wise man glory in his wisdom, neither let the mighty man glory in his strength, let not the rich man glory in his riches, but let him that glorieth glory in this that he understandeth and knoweth Me, that I am the Lord, which exerciseth loving-kindness, judgment, and righteousness, in the earth: for in these things I delight, saith the Lord" (ix. 23-24).

The Old Testament history and literature is the record of that supreme discovery of the ultimate nature of the Universe. It led inevitably to the most sweeping Monotheism, for there can only be one Highest, and in the very nature of the case the morally ideal One must be intolerant of gods or godlings on a lower ethical plane.

But the moment Monotheism came to its own, the problem of evil raised its formidable head. There is no problem of evil for animists or polytheists. There is no need for a devil, it has been caustically said, in the pagan religions, seeing that his functions were always efficiently discharged by one or other of the pantheon. But the moment the Hebrew came to believe in One Holy Righteous and Gracious God, he had the problem before him. How was he to explain the tragic elements in human life, disease, calamity, sorrow, labour, premature death? The first and fundamental idea of the Hebrew apologetic was that all the tragic elements in human life were due to the sin of man. At first this was applied with naïve simplicity of faith to the individual as well as to the national life. Whenever disaster befell any one, the conclusion was drawn that in some way that man had broken the law of Jehovah, and was suffering for his sins. But the facts of life were too strong for the theory, and so there arose for the Hebrews that specific form of the riddle of the world on which they spent so intense and prolonged a labour of thought, the problem of the sufferings of the righteous. Out of that turmoil of faith seeking to hold fast its supreme treasure, its master intuition of the moral perfection of its God, arose that great book which is the chief imaginative glory of Hebrew literature, the Book of Job. It was impossible after that to maintain the all too narrow theory of the earlier time. But Job gives no solution other than the appeal to the greatness of God's ways and the glory of the earth and heavens, and the assurance of faith that there must be an answer to the riddle. The Second Isaiah brings the solution a stage further with his marvellous intuition of the Suffering Servant and the vicarious character of the sufferings of the righteous. Finally, the assurance of the future life, in which all riddles are solved, comes glimmering up upon the horizon. But what we have in all this development of thought and emergence of new ideas of the first spiritual magnitude is not the abandonment of the original idea that the tragedies of human life are the result of human sin, but its expansion.

This is the central thought of the Hebrew

apologia, remaining constant through all the different stages through which it passes. Disease, premature death, poverty, famine, pestilence, national defeat, disaster, captivity, all the ills to which flesh is heir are constantly described in the Old Testament as due to man's folly and sin. The Hebrew never accepts them as part of the unchangeable nature of things. He is persuaded that they have no permanent place in God's world, and that they ought not to be, and would not be if only men with all their hearts turned to God. What is of capital importance for our present inquiry, they have no place in the coming Messianic order.

This fundamental idea is held with astonishing tenacity through the entire course of Hebrew literature. Its roots, of course, lie deep in the central thing in his religion, his idea of God, as perfectly ethical and as Almighty. Holding this faith he could not do other than interpret history as manifesting God. He must find God's character disclosed in what he believed to be God's providence.

Now, whatever we may think of this interpretation of life, it obviously conserved certain truths of the utmost importance. It enabled Israel to maintain an unquenchable vitality and courage throughout the tremendous discipline of its history, because it enabled it to hold fast the faith that God was really on the side of life and progress.

Here is the profound contrast between Indian and Hebrew thought, the pessimism of the one and the fundamental optimism of the other. The moment we come to believe that the evils of life are irremovable except by the escape from life, we doom ourselves either to stoical resignation or to ascetic mysticism. But if we believe that these evils are removable by the escape from sin, we enter, as did the Hebrews, on a long and ascending pathway of progress and hope, impelled by the faith that the nature of things is on our side.

We do not owe this idea to the story of the Fall. Rather do we owe the story of the Fall to the hold which the Hebrew idea had on the mind and soul of the nation. It is the mythical embodiment of a fundamental faith. Rightly understood, in fact, the main intention of the Fall story is not so much to show how sin entered the world, as to show how labour, weariness, pain, and death found a lodgment in God's world. It expresses the radical Hebrew faith that these tragic shadows are not part of the enduring substance of things as God ordained them. They are alien elements which have entered from without by the unbelief and weakness of man. The tempter wins a lodgment by inspiring mistrust in God. We have here surely the obverse of the Old Testament valuation of faith as the supreme virtue, and the very tragedy of the story is the product of that fundamental optimism of the Hebrew faith which lies at the heart of all true Theism.

III. The Spirit of God

The third Old Testament idea which underlies the Gospel story is that of the Spirit of God. We must, of course, dispel from our minds the thought of any real anticipation, at this early stage of revelation, of the Holy Spirit as a personality. The Old Testament conception is that of a Divine Potency, God in creative action in nature and in human life. The Hebrews had a much broader idea of the range of the action of the Spirit of God than is the case in our current religion. We think of the action of the Divine Spirit as confined strictly to the moral and spiritual life, but they thought of the Spirit as working along the whole range of human activities, bodily, mental, and spiritual. In general the action of the Spirit is thought of as theocratic. All special gifts that pertain to the furtherance of Israel's highest life, the genius of Aholiab and Bezaleel, who designed the Tabernacle, of the heroes and judges whom God raised up to preserve the independence of Israel, of the rulers who governed it and the prophets who purified its religion, are ascribed to the vitalising powers of the Spirit. But it is a natural extension of this principle to find the action of the Spirit everywhere in the world, for the world exists for the coming of the Kingdom of God.

In his striking book on *The Spirit in the New Testament*, Professor Scott points out that the idea of the Spirit as operative in the natural world finds its chief expression in the opening chapter of Genesis, where the Spirit of God is depicted as brooding on the face of the waters of primeval chaos, and calling into being the ordered ranks of being, and finally the ascending grades of life, vegetative, animal, and human.[8]

[8] *Cf.* Bergson's *Élan vital.* Is there any racial inheritance traceable here?

In particular is this the case with the wonders of life. Man's whole life is thought of as sustained by the Spirit of God, which animates and sustains in being his physical organism. The author of the Book of Job declares, "If He gather unto Himself His spirit, all flesh shall perish together" (Job xxxiv. 14, 15). We have here the same idea as is expressed in Genesis vi. 3: "My spirit shall not always strive with man forever, for that he also is flesh: yet shall his days be an hundred and twenty years." Taken in its context the passage obviously means that human life only exists by the indwelling of the Spirit within the human frame, what we would to-day call the anabolic force of life prevailing over the katabolic forces of decay.

In the 104th Psalm the Spirit appears as the vivifying influence in all creatures. "These wait all upon Thee . . . Thou takest away their breath, they die and return to the dust. Thou sendest forth Thy spirit, they are created; and Thou renewest the face of the earth" (Ps. civ. 27, 29, 30). The idea sometimes is that all forms of life are derived from the spirit. "They have all one spirit, and man hath no pre-eminence over the beasts." Elsewhere it is man alone to whom life is communicated by the Spirit. "My life is yet within me and the spirit of God is in my nostrils" (Job xxvii. 3). "But there is a spirit in man. The breath of the Almighty giveth them understanding" (Job xxxii. 8). "The Spirit of God hath made me and the breath of the Almighty giveth me life" (Job xxxiii. 4). Life as it exists in man would seem to be regarded as something of higher nature which has entered for a time into an earthly being. At death it returns to its Divine source, "to God who gave it" (Eccles. xii. 7; *cf.* Job xxxiv. 14).[9]

IV

The fourth Old Testament idea in the background of the thought of the Gospels is that of the Messianic Kingdom. In this Hebrew "Utopia," as it has been called, we find all the three thoughts of the Divine grace, of the moral order of the world, and of the Spirit presupposed and blended, fused together by that passionate vitality of faith and hope which is the very finest spirit of Israel. Its roots lie deep in the people's faith in the abiding Covenant grace of God. It was impossible for the true Israel to believe in the defeat of the purpose of its God, or to be content with the condition into which its own sins had brought it. Indian thought, face to face with the eternal riddle of the world, taught escape from the whole tremendous coil of evil for the individual by the way of Thought, as in the Vedanta; Stoicism, in the wide and dreary prison of the world, also sought deliverance for the individual by teaching indifference to fortune. But by virtue of its faith in the Covenant Israel sought its deliverance by other roads. Its Theistic faith compelled it to trace its own tragic fortunes not to any necessity in the scheme of the world, but to its own misuse of its freedom. The roots of its tragedy

[9] E. F. Scott, *The Spirit in the New Testament*, pp. 38, 39.

were not in God's world but in itself. They were therefore removable. There is a fundamental and far-reaching difference here. The view of things which denies sin is really, paradoxical as it may seem, far less hopeful than that which frankly admits the verdict of conscience. If man is the determinate victim of the world, then there is no hope for him save in submission. If he has departed from the true order of the world, or has not yet reached it, the whole outlook is incomparably more hopeful: the tragedy is in principle removable, there is hope in God.

So in the Theism of Israel this hope found expression in the idea of the Messianic Kingdom. This hope, which gleams intermittently through the prophetic writings and in the prophetic histories, finds very varied forms of expression which need not be dwelt on at this point in any detail. But in every form the deliverance is conceived of as coming from the grace of God. In Jeremiah it takes form in the great idea of a new Covenant, less outward and legal, more comprehensive and inward, wrought in the hearts of men by the power of God. The coming deliverance is primarily thought of as a reconciliation and reunion of the nation with God. In Isaiah, Israel, set free from its foes to worship its God, is thought of as in the foreground with the assenting nations of the world around it. But the outward curse is broken also. Sorrow, disease, and death disappear with sin in the highest forms of the Messianic hope. The life of heaven, in a word, comes to earth. This deliverance is always thought of as coming from the grace of

God, but the way can be prepared for it by repentance, obedience, and faith.

In many of the relevant passages the deliverance is thought of as coming by a personal Deliverer, the Messiah or Anointed of the Lord. He is conceived of as richly endowed with the life-giving Divine Spirit, and through His mediation that Spirit is poured out on men.

Here we have already, as it were, projected on the screen of the future the outlines of the Figure whom we see in the Gospels.

We have been describing the four Hebrew presuppositions, but our inquiry would be incomplete if we did not ask the further question, What changes happened to this picture in the Jewish version of Hebrew religion? Changes there were, but they do not seem to me to affect in any material way the broad outlines of the picture which has been sketched. The piety of the Old Covenant remains, but becomes more legal under the influence of Scribe and Pharisee. Yet faith in the Covenant God of Israel remains as the essential root of the Jewish piety. However burdened that faith may be, it persists, and great emphasis is laid, for example, upon its power to hasten the coming of the Messianic Age, a point of great importance, as we shall see presently when we come to the study of the Gospels.

The old and deeply rooted belief in the association of sin with tragedy remains and is deepened. Every true Jew believed in the judgments of God, and in the deep association of sin and premature death, death being the reflex of sin. The hope in the immortality and blessedness of the righteous, which was so prominent in the Jewish period, grows. Finally, the idea of the Messianic reign is emphasised, and, as in the earlier Scriptures, is always conceived of not only as the reign of holiness and righteousness, and the saints who embody these virtues, but as a time when the curses of death and disease are abolished, when the alien yoke of the heathen is broken, and the whole dark kingdom of evil, with the sway of the devil and his angels, is finally overthrown.

This Jewish version of the Hebrew solution of the riddle of the world is the background of all the life and thought of the Gospels, and it is in this setting only that the narratives of our Lord's great deeds and their place in His whole revelation can really be understood.

We are not concerned here with the truth of that view, or how far it is believable by modern men. That question will arise at a later stage. At present we are concerned simply with the question of what that view in its completeness really is. Our inquiry is historical and exegetical, and is the necessary preliminary to these later stages. It may be that the view which will finally emerge from our historical discussion is more believable and has more significance for our faith and life than either of the two theories which have been examined in an earlier chapter.

CHAPTER III

THE GOSPEL MIRACLES

We are now in a better position to understand the view of the signs of Jesus which is uniformly held by the Synoptic Evangelists. In this volume I have confined myself in the main to the Synoptic Gospels for exegetical proof of the positions advanced. There are in the Fourth Gospel traces of the purely evidential view, but these, it seems to me, have been gravely exaggerated. The broad general view is practically the same as that in the Synoptics, and in certain points is even more strongly stated. But discussion of the Fourth Gospel can only be carried out in view of its place at the end of the Apostolic age and the development of Apostolic thought. That the Synoptic Gospels have a perfectly clear and consistent view of their own, and that that view is different from both the Traditional and the Modernist views, I hope to make clear in this part of our argument. I do not suppose that almost any competent scholar will so far to-day question the main drift of what has been said above. Now for our further purpose it is not necessary at this point to go into the critical question of the sources of the Synoptic Gospels. It could, I believe, be easily shown that the view in question is that taken in all the sources, in Q, in the primitive Mark document, and in the additional matter used in the First and Third Gospels alike.

For clearness I propose to take the Gospel according to S. Matthew, as it is here that the general view comes most impressively to light.

What is that general view? It is that in Jesus Christ the Kingdom has already come actually and potentially, that the "signs" are manifestations of the Kingdom, and that they are wrought by the Spirit of God through the ideal faith of the Founder and in response to the faith of those who, through Him, enter into the Kingdom. As such they are anticipations and proleptic manifestations of the Kingdom in its perfection when the reign of sin and death shall have been finally broken. The author of the First Gospel, instead of the term, the Kingdom of God, uses the term, the Kingdom of Heaven. The "signs" of the Kingdom of Heaven are manifestations of the heavenly life, fragments of heaven in the life of time.

The first point to notice here is the extraordinary emphasis put by Christ everywhere in the Synoptic narratives on the necessity of faith. This is the element in His teaching which is as it were blurred and half suppressed under both the Traditionalist and Modernist views. It is necessary to go into this with some detail, for its truly remarkable character seems to me to-day to be as a rule quite inadequately recognised, and to carry far-reaching consequences for Christian theology.

The First Gospel, then, after the introductory sections dealing with the ancestry and infancy of

Jesus, and carrying the narrative to Nazareth, tells of the appearing and mission of the Baptist, the descent of the Spirit, and the Temptation. Then comes the announcement of the coming of the Kingdom, "Repent ye, for the Kingdom of Heaven is at hand." The call of the first two disciples follows, and the first missionary journey with its broadcast healings of disease—"healing all manner of disease and all manner of sickness among the people." Then comes the Sermon on the Mount, containing material, probably, that is drawn from several periods in our Lord's ministry. What we are concerned with mainly here, however, is S. Matthew's general presentation of the history, and it is noteworthy that he begins with the simple announcement of the coming advent of the Kingdom, and the record of its characteristic signs, the signs that people of that age and creed would naturally expect from a Deliverer from the sway of the evil one over the bodies and minds of men. Then comes the fuller unfolding of the kind of life which the Kingdom demands.

Then follow the eighth and ninth chapters, which are almost entirely taken up with the records of the healing of disease, the story of the leper (leprosy being for the Jew, on account of its malignity, much what cancer is to-day for the Western peoples), of the centurion's servant, of Peter's wife's mother, and of the scene in Capernaum, "at even when the sun did set," of the stilling of the storm, of the healing of the Gadarene demoniac, of another paralytic, of Jairus's daughter, of the woman with the issue of blood, of the two blind men, and of a dumb demoniac. The section closes with another journey, like the first, of broadcast healing and of teaching. Not content with this, Jesus finally calls the complete circle of the twelve disciples, and gives them authority over unclean spirits to cast them out and to heal all manner of disease and all manner of sickness, transferring, as it were, His powers to His followers.

Now let us for a moment revert to the details of these stories. Nine of them are concerned with the healing of diseased persons. In the first the leper's faith in the power of Jesus to help him is emphasised. In the story of the centurion's servant the faith of the centurion is the real point of the story. Jesus marvels at it, and sees in it the promise of the ingathering of the Gentiles into the Kingdom. He then cures the servant, explicitly associating that cure with the centurion's faith. Nothing is said of faith in the next narrative, the healing of Peter's wife's mother, but it is presupposed, as the appeal for aid comes from the household of His leading disciple. Then comes the stilling of the storm on the lake and the rebuke of the disciples for their alarm, "Why are ye fearful, O ye of little faith?" There was no reason for alarm, they would neither sink nor drown.

In the case of the Gadarene demoniac, nothing is said of faith. Indeed, in all such cases of possession, faith is impossible on the part of the patient, and is never required of him. Again, in the next story, the healing of the palsied man, the motive is the same as elsewhere. "Jesus, seeing their faith," announces the man's forgiveness, and having given the greater gift, proceeds to give the less, and heals him.

Then comes the very remarkable double story of the raising from the dead of the ruler's daughter, and the healing of the woman with the issue of blood. In both cases, in the faith of Jairus and in the faith of the woman, the principle is emphasised, and in the second, Christ says in so many words to the woman, " Thy faith hath made thee whole." Next comes the healing of the two blind men. Here we are told that Christ asked of them if they had faith, and that in bestowing sight He said to them, " According to your faith, be it unto you."

The last of the " signs " in these chapters is the healing of another demoniac which comes under the rule referred to above.

Now the meaning of this whole section is surely perfectly clear. Yet, if it had been rightly considered, the Traditional theory of miracle, which, as we have seen, regards the miracles of Jesus as evidential portents of mere Divine power, could hardly have come into being. Such portents elsewhere are explicitly refused by Jesus. They correspond to the " signs " for which the Jews asked, and of which He said, " An evil and adulterous generation seeketh after a sign, and there shall no sign be given it save the sign of Jonas the prophet."

The " signs " of these two chapters are something much more than portents, they are revelations of the presence of the Kingdom of God, not, as has been said, seals attached to the document, but parts of the document itself. To those who saw and understood them, they were revelations of the ideal will of God for man, and of man's ideal destiny, assurances, also, that God was with Jesus to make that ideal a reality even here in the world of time.

Of capital importance, also, is the continual emphasis given by Christ to faith as the condition of these "signs." There is no evading the clear testimony of the Synoptic Gospels as to this point in the great majority of the miracles of healing. Yet on the Traditional theory it is impossible to account for this. On that theory, which emphasises Divine Power as the essential evidential point, all such human co-operation in the "signs" detracts from the Divine wonder. The inability of Jesus to work any mighty works in Nazareth for instance does not harmonise at all with the view on which the signs are signs above all of the unconditional Divine power of the Son of God.

Hence the prevalence of the Traditional view has had unhappy effects in blinding many interpreters of the Gospels to the remarkable and far-reaching character of our Lord's teaching about the creative power of faith. But on the view of the signs of Christ supported in these pages, it is easy to see why just this emphasis should be laid on man's co-operation with God, or rather man's receptiveness to God. The Old Testament view of faith being what it was, this is precisely what we should expect.

We have here, in fact, a development of the view which we find in the Old Testament throughout. The announcement of the Kingdom corresponds to the founding of the Covenant. It is the new and final advance of God's grace to men, a great deepening and widening of the old relation, initiated by God with the old Israel. But as in that Old Covenant, all its blessings are mediated through faith. Faith is the root virtue of both, and that is why throughout the whole teaching of Jesus there is an incessant call above all other things for faith, with the continually repeated assurance that there is nothing in the way of goodness that faith cannot attain, and nothing in the way of blessing in breaking the mortal powers of evil that it cannot achieve. The essential point to notice here is that, according to these Gospels and their presentation of the teaching of Jesus, both the realm within the soul and the realm without, both the sin within man and the tragic element in human life, are regarded as alike spheres for conquest by the victorious energy of faith. Modern theological thought has held to the first, but hesitates as to the second, or even denies the power of faith over the physical world at all. The far-reaching importance of this will become obvious as we proceed with our discussion. We return now from this digression to our examination of the narrative in the Gospel of S. Matthew.

Having made this point as to faith and its inseparable and vital connection with the great deeds of Jesus, the Evangelist does not deem it necessary at every stage in the rest of the narratives of the signs to make it explicit. It is not necessary to do so in these highly condensed narratives. But none the less the idea runs through the whole story, and comes again and again to the surface.

The section of the Gospel which follows that containing the Sermon on the Mount and the two great chapters recounting the mighty deeds of Jesus, opens with the calling of the twelve and a discourse to them: then follows the message from the Baptist asking them for assurance as to His Divine mission. "Art thou He that should come, or look we for another?" In effect this was an appeal for some sign that the Kingdom of God had really come.

Jesus goes right to the heart of the matter at once. He does not, as He might well have done, send John a personal assurance of the sympathy and admiration for him that He unquestionably felt, and expressed to His own disciples immediately after. That would have been but superficial comfort for the great spirit of the Baptist. He gives eloquent proof of His appreciation of the greatness of John by His deeds. "In that hour," we are told, in the parallel passage in S. Luke, Jesus "cured many of diseases and plagues and evil spirits, and on many that were blind He bestowed sight." And He answered and said unto them, "Go your way and tell John what things which ye do hear and see: the blind receive their sight, and the lame walk, the lepers are cleansed, and the deaf hear, and the dead are raised up, the poor have good tidings preached to them. And blessed is he, whosoever shall find none occasion of stumbling in Me" (Matt. xi. 4-6). It may seem to a superficial reader as if we had here simply the portent theory of miracle back again. But that is not so. Not even for John would He have given a useless astronomical sign to prove the truth of His teaching. He does better than give him convincing external evidence of the truth of His teaching about the Kingdom. He actually shows him the Kingdom as present in the healed bodies and renewed spirits of men.

The "things which they see" are obviously the acts of healing, with a reference back to the two preceding chapters of such signs; "the things which they hear" are the verbal teaching as to God, man, and the Gospel of the Kingdom, with a reference back to the Sermon on the Mount.

In the fourteenth chapter of S. Matthew we have the teaching as to faith still further illustrated in the story of Christ walking upon the water. When He comes to the disciples across the sea, Peter desires to come to Him out of the boat. And when he turns his gaze away from Jesus, and realises the fury of the storm, he begins to sink. Whereupon Jesus says to him, "O thou of little faith, wherefore didst thou doubt?" The implication is clear. Had he had faith like his Master, he would have been in no danger from the mortal powers of nature.

The next story of healing is that of the Syrophœnician woman. Surely the whole point of this story is that when Christ finds that vital thing, faith, even in a woman outside the historic Covenant, He grants to her the hidden wealth of the Kingdom even as to His own countrymen. We have here the germ of the whole Pauline universalism. "O woman, great is thy faith. Be it done unto thee even as thou wilt. And her daughter was healed from that hour."

This follows the story of the feeding of the five thousand, and then for the second time Jesus refuses to work a mere marvel and disposes beforehand of the type of miracle beloved by eighteenth-century apologists and mediæval legend mongers, with the austere words, " An evil and adulterous generation seeketh after a sign."

The next healing is that of the epileptic boy. Here Jesus is reported as filled with sorrow and condemnation that such misery should not have been removed already. " O faithless and perverse generation! How long shall I be with you, how long shall I suffer you! Bring him hither to Me!"

Then follows a pregnant paragraph which, even had it stood alone, would have been absolutely conclusive as to the main point which I am seeking to establish. The disciples, after their failure to heal the demoniac, come to Him and raise the central issue, " Why could not we cast it out ? " The answer is equally direct. Jesus does not say, " Because of God's immutable decree." He says, " Because of your little faith, for verily I say unto you, If ye have faith as a grain of mustard seed, ye shall say unto this mountain, Remove hence to yonder place: and it shall remove, and nothing shall be impossible unto you."

This is one of the few places where the briefer narrative of S. Mark is even fuller than that of the other two on the question at issue. According to this narrative the father says to Jesus, " If thou canst do anything, have compassion on us and help us. And Jesus saith unto him, If thou canst. Believe! All things are possible to him that believeth. Straightway the father of the child cried out and said, I believe, help Thou my unbelief!" The heart of the tragedy being now laid bare, "the boy was cured from that hour."

It is surely now perfectly clear that there is one great principle running through all these sayings about faith, that the Synoptic Gospels regard the whole realm of sin within the heart and of tragedy from without which strike at and poison the life of man as not being part of the unchangeable order of God. They are intruders, and since Christ has come, they can be dispelled by faith. Take, for instance, the crucial case of disease. Jesus never seems to have hesitated in treating it as something alien to the Kingdom of Heaven, and to have struck at it whenever He found faith to be healed.

We cannot otherwise account for the narratives of what I have called broadcast healing, the waves of life giving energy that seemed to go out of Him among the multitudes of sick who gathered round Him. Indeed, He seems, as in Nazareth, at least to have wished to strike at it where the general unbelief prevented it. There is not one single instance recorded in which He refused the appeal of a sick man on the ground that it was God's will that he should continue to suffer. And unquestionably He approved of, indeed delighted in that will to be healed and faith to be healed, and gloried in the powers of healing that God had given Him. It is, of course, true that He put far more importance on the healing of the soul than on the healing of the body, and where

He found that the work of the latter prevented the practice of the former, or encroached on the time essential for the keeping open of the channel of communion with His Father, He retired from the practice of healing, or forbade the healed to spread the news of it, and to create unmanageable or intrusive crowds of wonder seekers. But to exaggerate this wholly intelligible action into a certain disparagement on His part of the healing gift is an absolute travesty of the plain meaning of the narratives. It is perfectly clear that He gloried in the work of healing the bodies as well as the souls of men, and that He regarded the overthrow of disease as an essential part of His mission and of His manifestation of the Kingdom. It may be said that all this is quite alien to our modern ways of thinking. Even if it were, we have no right when we are dealing historically with the documents to impose our modern ideas upon them. There is only one question that we have the right, as honest inquirers, to ask: What did this writer think and what did he mean to say? That is the first principle of all sound interpretation. In this case the thoughts and the meaning of the Evangelists, I submit, are plain.

But if this be admitted, the question may fairly be asked, Is this way of looking at, for example, disease in any material way different from the way of any good physician to-day? He is always out against disease on principle, and never hesitates when he is face to face with any malady, to strike at it by any means in his power. To him it is simply an evil to be attacked and destroyed by drugs, by diet, by treatment of all kinds, by surgery, or by sanitation, in a word by the liberating in every way possible of the vital powers, the *vis medicatrix naturæ*. His assumption always is that disease is against sound nature, and therefore something which ought not to be. He never asks whether it might not be for his patient's spiritual good to remain physically diseased. Neither, so far as I can see, did Jesus. The only real difference is that the modern physician attacks it, or used to attack it (for a change has of late been obviously coming over the scene) from the side of the body only. The New Testament men, and above all Christ Himself, believed it could be attacked more powerfully from within, and put their hopes on reinforcing indefinitely the powers of the spirit. And the whole tendency in modern medicine, if a layman in medicine has read the position rightly, has been for the modern mind to make a tentative advance towards the older view. The whole development of psycho-therapeutics is significant. It is much too early in that movement as yet to lay down any hard and fast views as to the limits beyond which it may not go. Modern medical thought and practice is not a fixed, but a moving thing. Sober thought may yet revert to Luther's saying, that if we have faith enough to be healed, there is no disease from which we may not recover. The dictum of the *British Medical Journal*, that there is no tissue of the human body wholly removed from the influence of spirit, is at least a significant step in that direction. We may close our brief review of the teaching of the Synoptic Gospels on the vital part that faith plays in the signs of Jesus by saying that it should be noted that Christ says that great faith enables great deeds to be done, that too scant a faith and still more its absence can check even His own activity of blessing, and that in one instance He even says, "According to your faith be it unto you." The strongest saying as to the power of faith to change the courses of things and overthrow all that stands in the way of the Kingdom of Heaven is repeated in these Gospels in different contexts and in slightly varying forms of expression. In S. Matthew, as we have seen, when the disciples ask the reason of their failure to cast out the evil spirit, He replies, "Because of your little faith," and continues, "Verily I say unto you, if ye have faith as a grain of mustard seed ye shall say unto this mountain, Remove hence to yonder place, and it shall remove, and nothing shall be impossible to you." In Luke (xvii. 5), shrinking from the call to unlimited forgiveness, the disciples say, "Increase our faith"; and the Lord said, "If ye have faith as a grain of mustard seed, ye would say unto this sycamine tree, Be thou rooted up and be thou planted in the sea: and it would have obeyed you." It is true that, as the alarmed commentators laboriously point out, we have here vivid Oriental metaphor. But the metaphor *means* something for all that. Just how much it means, the record of the signs, the victories over disease and death, the feeding of the multitudes, and the control of the storm and the waters give abundant proof. When we are at the task of interpreting what Matthew or Luke really believed that Jesus meant, we have to remember what the same writers report Him to have done.

We pass on now to the further question as to whether the Evangelists mean us to look upon this same principle of faith as enabling Christ to work His own "signs," or whether we are to think of them as signs rather of some inherent and unconditional Divine energy, or simply apart from His faith altogether, as sovereign acts of God, who uses Him as instrument of His creative power and love and wisdom.

In pursuance of this inquiry, then, we have now to consider the question of our Lord's teaching about prayer as we find it set before us in the Synoptic Gospels, and in particular His view of the power of the right kind of petitionary prayer.

In nothing is the contrast between the New Testament and the prevailing theory and practice of our own day more sharply in contrast than as to the power of petitionary prayer. We shall consider in another context the reasons for this, which are deeply rooted in much of the thought of our time. The pressure on the religious, and in particular the Christian thought of our time, of the idea of an unalterable course of nature, has been so great as to make this teaching of Jesus almost mute, to suppress its meaning so as to make us even unconscious of its force. In an impressive passage of his book on *The Kingdom and the Messiah*, Professor E. F. Scott shows that Jesus believed that the coming and victory of the Kingdom could be accelerated by the believing and importunate prayers of the faithful, and says, "By His welcome of importunacy in prayer, Jesus implied that God Himself accepted it and would refuse nothing to an insistent faith. This aspect of the thought of Jesus can be seen even more clearly in His explicit sayings about the power of prayer. Prayer, as He conceives it, is much more than a waiting on God, in passive self-surrender to an inevitable will. The prayer of faith will assure its own fulfilment. 'Ask and ye shall receive; seek and ye shall find; knock and it shall be opened unto you.' The will of God is not wholly fixed and unalterable. It is the will of our Father, who is aware of our needs and longings, and who desires that we should plead with Him and prevail. By granting us access to Himself in prayer, He has given us control over the mightiest of all powers. We have the right to use this power, and to win for ourselves the interposition of God even when He seems most unwilling. Jesus Himself was strong through prayer. He believed that by means of it He had the might of God to support Him; and He sought to impart His own assurance to His disciples."[1]

It is unnecessary to give all the passages illustrating this conception of the power of prayer to influence and change the ordinary course both of nature and of the circumstances of human life. It will be sufficient to call attention to the remarkable catena of passages in the eleventh chapter of S. Luke. Let us consider the sequence here. Jesus, being asked for a method in prayer, gives His disciples "the Lord's Prayer," which includes not only prayer for inward and "spiritual" blessings,

[1] *Cf.* Appendix C.

but for the historic coming of the greatest of all events, the Kingdom of God, which, as we have seen, includes the outer as well as the inner blessings, the abolition of both sin within and tragedy without, and also for the plain obvious outward good of " daily bread."

Then comes the parable of the importunate friend, of which the point obviously is the persistence of the friend, the refusal to take a refusal.

Then comes the triad of imperatives. Ask, seek, knock. You are to ask, and if you do not get what you want by asking, you are to do everything you can to find out the causes of the rejection, and finally you are to beat at the closed door!

Then comes the sweeping statement of the principle, " Every one that asketh, receiveth; and he that seeketh findeth; to him that knocketh it shall be opened." Finally comes the saying that clinches the whole, compares God with man, and asks how if a human father can be trusted to satisfy plain human wants, we can distrust the willingness of the Almighty Father to give the Holy Spirit to them that ask Him. In the parallel passage in S. Matthew, we have the reading " good things " instead of the Holy Spirit. The difference, however, is immaterial, for, according to the Synoptics, the Holy Spirit is the all-inclusive gift, including ideally the whole range of the " miraculous."

Now, if we let this remarkable group of passages with its crescendo of promises have its full force upon our minds, we get some estimate of His idea of the range and power of ideal human prayer. It is a window into His own inner life, into the kind of faith which He had in God, and the expectations of His succour in which He lived. It is clear that this kind of prayer presupposes, and has as its animating spirit the kind of faith by which He wrought His own mighty works. If all this be true of ideal prayer, then we can understand how Jesus was able to heal the sick, and still the storm, and raise the dead. The teaching and the deeds fit one another like hand and glove.

He is obviously dealing with the same kind of force as He was thinking of when He said that if the disciples had faith as a grain of mustard seed they would move mountains. He is thinking of prayer electrically charged, as it were, with faith, of faith as expressing itself in believing prayer. Indeed He repeatedly and expressly associates the prayer which prevails with God with faith. It is not mere obstinate despairing importunity of which He is really thinking, the mechanical repetition of despairing petitions to an unwilling God. "Whatsoever ye ask in prayer, believing, ye shall receive." According to His wont in teaching, He isolates and emphasises one aspect after another of the idea He is seeking to express. He speaks now of importunacy, and now of faith as the essential thing. But to get at His whole meaning we have to combine both the aspects in a whole, and therefore in ideal prayer we have to think of importunacy as starting from and as charged with faith, and of faith as persisting against apparent rebuff, as the Syrophœnician woman did.

But this is not all. The prayer that prevails is a prayer charged with hope. "Believe that ye have received the things ye ask for, and ye shall have them." We have to "expect great things from God" if we are to "attempt great things for God."

And, finally, prevailing prayer must be charged with love. "When ye stand praying, forgive if ye have aught against any." "Verily I say unto you, if two of you shall agree as touching anything that ye shall ask, it shall be done for them of My Father which is in heaven." The only thing that can make men really forgiving, and can completely unite their wills, is love.

If we let all these passages have their full and natural weight with us, it is surely impossible to evade the conclusion that He is letting us into the secret of His own "miracle"-working powers.

He does His mighty deeds by prayer, sustained and carried home by His unique faith, hope, and love. The roots of His unique power over nature lie therefore in His unique spiritual character, not in His metaphysical Divinity, but in His perfect humanity. All this seems irresistibly implied in His sayings about prayer. Have we over and above this any explicit assertion that His supernatural powers come through prayer? We have one such unambiguous saying in the Synoptic Gospels.

At the moment of His arrest He rebukes the violence of Peter, and tells him that there is no need for it, that if He wished He could at any moment deliver Himself. "Thinkest thou that I cannot now pray to My Father and He should presently give Me more than twelve legions of angels?" That this belief that our Lord's works were wrought by prayer was the underlying view of the early community and the Apostolic circle is still further evidenced by the fact that the Fourth Gospel, which is the most explicit of them all on the inherent Divinity of our Lord, ascribes His greatest work, the raising of Lazarus, to the direct prayer of Christ to His Heavenly Father. What was believed to be true of this " sign " must clearly also have been true of all the rest.

The cumulative case seems to me irresistible. The Gospel theory of the " miracles " of Jesus is that they are the answers of God to the prayers of the Ideal Son, the Man who is the supreme instance, in history, of Faith, Hope, and Love; and they say with unambiguous plainness that that ideal Man invited His disciples to similar enterprises of faith, encouraging them to believe that in proportion to their faith would be the manifestation of God's order, the revelation of man's life as God meant it to be.

But we have not yet completed our survey of the thought of the Gospels. We have been looking at the signs of Jesus mainly from the human side, and so have dwelt upon the moral and spiritual conditions of their appearance. We have now to complete that survey by taking into account their origin in God, the supreme Creative Power by whom they were ultimately wrought. We have therefore, finally, to consider at this point the Synoptic and early Apostolic idea of the Holy Spirit.

We are concerned, first of all, with the idea of the Spirit of God as it appears in the Evangelists.

In Professor Scott's admirable volume on *The Holy Spirit in the New Testament*, he draws a distinction between our Lord's own view of the Spirit and that of the Evangelists, who, he thinks, read back into the Gospels the thoughts and experiences of the Apostolic age, when, as is universally admitted, the idea of the Spirit acquires a new prominence. This part of his argument does not seem to me at all convincing. Indeed, of the sayings of Jesus about the Holy Spirit he admits so much to be original, that it seems unnecessary to reject the rest. But in any case, what we are here concerned with is the view set forth in the Gospels themselves, and as to this there seems no ground for dispute.

In the period between the Testaments the idea of the Spirit had been in some eclipse. It was an age of the law and the scribe rather than of prophecy; and the interest of Jewish thought, so far as it was active on the subject of the continued action of God upon the world, had been absorbed by the fascinating Logos conception, and the alluring hope which it held out of harmonious union between the finest contemporary Greek thought and the wealth of spiritual genius and experience contained in the Hebrew tradition. We can understand this when we think of the eagerness with which progressive Christians looked in the last generation upon the theory of Evolution, and that with which younger thinkers are in our day turning to the idea of the Unconscious Mind.

But the faith that the Messiah would be richly endowed with the Spirit of God, and that through

Him that Spirit would be abundantly poured forth on all the faithful, persisted.[2] The source of this plenitude of Divine life, according to the Psalms of Solomon, is the Messiah's fear of God, a reverent trust in Him, from which comes all His confidence and hope (xvii. 34, 39).[3] The life of the devout Jew was too deeply rooted in the Old Testament for the faith in the coming of the Divine Spirit to have been lost. These Scriptures, as we have seen, anticipated with the coming of the Messiah an outpouring of the Spirit of God, the Spirit which raised all man's higher activities to their noblest power, and which lived at the very springs even of man's physical life.

Into this situation came the apparition and the call of John the Baptist. We have now briefly to review the teaching of the Evangelists on the relation of the Holy Spirit to the signs of Jesus. We shall follow here for convenience the same method as in dealing with the prominence given by these writers to faith. There is no real divergence between the Evangelists in this matter any more than there is any real difference on the matter of faith. They all obviously take the same view. But just as S. Matthew lays peculiar emphasis

[2] "In the future must all the devout be bearers of the Spirit. . . . It will be the task of the Messiah to pour forth the Spirit on all believing ones" (Testt. Lev. xviii. 7; Jude xxiv. 2); *cf.* Sibylline Oracles, iii. 582; Bousset, *Religion des Judenthums im N.T. Zeitalter*, 2nd ed., p. 453.

[3] Quoted by Volz, *Jüdische Eschatologie*: "The source of the Messiah's power is the fear of God. His confidence is in the Lord, therefore can no one do anything against Him. His trust is not in horse or rider . . . but the Lord is His hope" (p. 232).

on faith, S. Luke lays peculiar emphasis on the Spirit, both in his Gospel and in the Acts, and so we shall take his narrative as exhibiting with emphasis the general view. In the introductory sections of this Gospel we have first the promise of the coming of the Baptist as one "filled with the Holy Spirit, even from his mother's womb." Then comes the story of the Annunciation and of the Virgin Birth by the power of the Spirit. The story of the mission of the Baptist follows. In his announcement of the coming of the Christ, he specifically describes His work as follows: "He shall baptise you with the Holy Spirit and with fire."

Then comes the Baptism of Jesus. "And it came to pass, when all the people were baptised, that Jesus also having been baptised, the heaven was opened, and the Holy Spirit in answer to His prayer descended in a bodily form as a dove upon Him, and a voice came out of heaven, Thou art My beloved Son, in Thee I am well pleased." This Baptism of the Spirit is obviously, as we shall see, the vital point in the whole narrative. It is probably the key to the story of the Temptation. Every Divine gift carries with it, as history shows, the possibility of the most tragic misuse, and that even the gift of the Divine Spirit carries with it temptations seems to be the point of the narrative. If that gift of the Spirit lay solely, as we sometimes suppose, in an exaltation of the moral and spiritual nature, it would be difficult to see how this could be the case; but if, as is our argument, it included control over the destroying and "evil" element in nature, and the power to work " signs " of that control, it is quite otherwise. Having emerged from the Temptation, Jesus (Luke iv. 14) returned " in the power of the Spirit " into Galilee. In Galilee, He comes into the synagogue, and declares the nature of His mission to His fellow-citizens.

It is decisive that in order to do this, He selects from the Old Testament writings the passage from Isaiah lxi. 1, 2: " The Spirit of the Lord is upon Me, because He anointed Me to preach good tidings to the poor: He hath sent Me to proclaim release to the captives, and recovering of sight to the blind, to set at liberty them that are bruised, to proclaim the acceptable year of the Lord." Taken in the context of His teaching and deeds, this is a clear statement that He regards not only His preaching, but His mighty deeds as created and sustained by the Spirit of the Lord.

The basal and inclusive idea being thus explicitly stated at the outset, there is no need for emphasising it in the particular narratives, any more than we saw to be the case when the Evangelists were speaking of faith as the condition of the " mighty works."

The next explicit reference to the Spirit is in x. 21, where we are told He " rejoiced in the Holy Spirit." The idea here is, clearly, that His ordinary experience is carried for the moment into an even higher zone of insight and gladness by the touch of the Spirit leading Him on to see new depths of the Divine.

The next is xi. 13, where S. Luke gives us a variant to S. Mark's rendering, " How much more shall your

Heavenly Father give the Holy Spirit to them that ask Him!" S. Luke probably supplies Holy Spirit for S. Matthew's "good things," as Dr Denney has suggested, simply because to him the Holy Spirit "is regarded as the inclusive gift of the Kingdom, containing in principle all its blessings."

A little later in the same chapter there is a curious variant on the other two Synoptics of an opposite kind. S. Matthew and S. Mark say, "If I, by the Spirit of God, cast out demons, then is the Kingdom of God come upon you." S. Luke, instead of "the Spirit of God," reads "the finger of God." The variation is of little moment, for there is abundant evidence that S. Luke, by the "finger of God," meant essentially the same as he means elsewhere when he speaks of the Spirit. The important point for our present purpose is that all three passages alike treat the "signs" of casting out demons, as proof that the Kingdom of God is already present, and that they are not wrought by Jesus, as a "second Jehovah," acting as it were from His own inherent strength, but as the medium through which the living energy of God is able to work among men.

The next direct reference is in the twelfth chapter, where we have the passage about the unpardonable sin. According to the Lucan version of this saying, the sin of blasphemy against the Holy Spirit is said to be worse than the sin involved in speaking against the Son of Man, and to carry him who commits it out of reach even of the forgiveness of God. We seem to have here already anticipated the Apostolic view of the gift of the Spirit, the culminating step in the progress of redemption, the end for which the Son of Man came, and lived and died and rose again. The Holy Spirit is as it were God's last and highest word to men, the word which finally interprets the Son of Man, which speaks in conscience, in man's ideals, and at its loudest and clearest in the fullest Christian experience. To have known that experience and to have destroyed it, is to kill the sense of hearing of the soul. The gravity of the warning is the measure of the supreme value put upon the gift of the Spirit. This seems to be the meaning of this difficult passage, and it is very hard to think that we have not here Christ's own words, and that we have not in them something prior to the Epistles. Yet if so, we have here implied in negative form the essence of the whole apostolic doctrine of the Spirit. The passage is followed immediately by the promise of supernatural guidance by the Spirit in all moments of emergency and danger. Nothing more is said directly of the Spirit until the close of the Gospel, where the disciples are told to wait in Jerusalem the fulfilment of the "promise of the Father," which is explained as the being "endued with power from on high."

We have here in this sequence of references, it may be granted, much less than is said in S. Matthew of the power of faith. But surely what is said is quite decisive.

The Baptism, with the descent of the Spirit upon Jesus, is, in the light of the passages which have been cited, meant to give the key to the whole story, the Divine explanation of the marvellous personality and deeds of Jesus. It takes in the Gospel of S. Luke the same place as is taken in the Acts by the narrative of Pentecost. It is as if the writer in the one case said this is what a man filled by the Spirit can do, and in the other this is what a Church baptised by the Spirit can do.

The Baptism is, further, the ultimate explanation of all the "signs" of Jesus. These are characteristic and creative works of the Spirit, the Spirit to which the later and greater Hebrew literature ascribed the origin and maintenance of life, the works of consecrated genius, and the highest ranges of insight, foresight, and the vision of God. It was fitting that that Spirit should be manifested in the healing of the blind, the opening of the deaf ears, the setting free of the paralysed, the insane, and the leper, and even in raising the dead. When the Spirit wrought this, it wrought according to its true genius and idea as surely as when it dispelled the diseases and the death of the soul, and brought men home to God.

To sum up the whole argument of these last two chapters, it seems to me quite clear that we have here a coherent organic unity of thought. It is quite impossible, given the Old Testament and Jewish presuppositions, to regard these signs of Jesus as something accidental and external to the rest of the record, if the teaching of the Old Testament and New is as I have represented it; and if Jesus were what the Gospels suppose Him to be, the ideally pure and representative Man, and as such the Founder of the new order, then it was essential that He should work just such "signs" (to speak broadly and generally) as they represent Him to have wrought. These signs, therefore, are integral parts of the revelation, and not adjuncts to it. They are revelations of the ideal purpose of God for mankind, and therefore of His character. They must therefore necessarily influence our idea of God. Inasmuch, also, as they imply the coming into the order of nature of powers that cannot be explained in terms of mere nature, they must inevitably affect our whole conception of the world. And, finally, as they are works wrought through the Perfect Man, and are meant by Him to be imitated by imperfect men, they must affect our conceptions of the possibilities of man, and the possibilities and range of prayer.

The Synoptics sometimes approach these signs from the human side, and speak of them as wrought through faith. But sometimes they go deeper, and speak of them as wrought by the Spirit. We are just to their whole conception only when we say that they were one and all wrought by the Spirit of God through the faith of man and, above all, through the faith of the Son of Man, "the leader and the perfection of faith" (Heb. xii. 2).

We have now completed this brief sketch of the Synoptic theory of the signs of Jesus. It is surely clear that we have here something quite different from and much more than the Traditional theory has any room for, something which is of moment for the whole system of Christian thought and life. But is it really a tenable view to-day, or has the progress of scientific knowledge rendered it a mere archaism, believable by no man touched by the modern spirit ?

This is the inquiry to which we must now address ourselves in the following chapters.

CHAPTER IV

SCIENCE AND RELIGION

We have in an earlier part of this volume shown that the miracles of our Lord are not an accidental but an organic part of that view of the world which we find in the Bible. The world according to the uniform witness of the Bible is created by God, is dependent on God, and is plastic in the hands of God. The last of these truths is the one which is most difficult for the modern mind to believe and to realise.

The difficulty has been created mainly by the rise and development of physical science, which appears to demand that the realm of physical nature shall be considered as rigid to all influences other than physical, in other words that it shall be regarded as a completely self-enclosed and self-explanatory system. This is what lies behind the whole conception of the Reign of Law and of the Uniformity of Nature.

What is meant by the term " self enclosed " and " self explanatory " ?

That view seems to many to imply that nature is absolutely rigid to any influence beyond itself. In other words, the entire realm of nature, by which I here mean the world to which we have access through the senses, is a self-enclosed and self-explanatory system, in which every event can be explained in terms of its physical antecedents and physical consequents. It is, of course, clear that if nature be of this type, it is absurd to suppose that there can be any intervening influence from a spiritual world deflecting or influencing any physical event whatever.

The whole literature of Revelation proceeds on quite another view. It invariably regards nature as a plastic medium through which God works out His purposes in the lives of free human spirits. The world to Him is, as it were, not like a gauntlet of steel, far less of stone, but like a silken glove.

This is the fundamental difficulty which the rise and development of modern science has created for personal religion in our modern world. The controversy over miracle is simply part of a much wider whole, and can only be understood in that larger context. The real matter at stake is the Christian doctrine of the world. We can put the issue more broadly still. It is, or rather it appears to be, between the scientific and the religious interpretation of life.

How far-reaching is this apparent clash between the scientific and the religious interpretation of life we can realise if we go into any one of our great public libraries, open to the public, according to the new system, in all its departments. On one side of a corridor we find textbooks of science in every one of which it is assumed as a matter of course that only physical forces are at work in its special domain—physics, chemistry, biology, geology, and so forth. We step over to the religious department, and we find there the unvarying assumption that God is at work as an efficient influence and causality throughout His world, as a Providence controlling not only humanity as a whole, but individual lives through natural incidents, and as a Divine Spirit changing the psychical life, and through it influencing alike men's bodies and their outer environment.

We seem to find, in a word, two different and conflicting interpretations of the world, the one impersonal, general, and abstract, which seeks everywhere for causality and law; the other, as William James has said, "personal and romantic." This, to-day, is the real "conflict between Science and Religion," a battle along the whole line, instead of such outpost affairs as the conflict between the scientific account of man's origin and history, and the Biblical narratives of the Garden of Eden, the six days of Creation, and so forth, about which our fathers were so deeply concerned. The settlement of such outpost skirmishes, and the drawing of a distinction between what is important and what is unimportant on either side has been hailed as a reconciliation between science and religion. I think all such rejoicings are premature until a clear understanding shall have been reached on the far deeper and wider issue. That such an understanding is in process of being realised is the ultimate argument of this chapter. But we have first to dispose of some of the premature attempts at a concordat which have been attempted and which still cumber the road to a final reconciliation. The older traditional apologetics, to begin with, drew a distinction between Divine providences and Divine answers to human prayer on the one hand, and miracles on the other. The former were in strict conformity with the "Reign of Law," whereas the latter were something more, they were direct interventions of God. The Divine action in the first two was illustrated by the action of a human father, who, it was assumed, could supervise and provide for his children without deflecting the system of natural "law." Miracle was something over and above this, to which there was nothing strictly parallel in ordinary human experience. The very fact that it was of this unique kind made it the more convincing as an unmistakable Divine confirmation of the truth of the accompanying revelation. The extension and tightening-up of the whole scientific conception of nature have made this older apologetic distinction obsolete. The Reign of Law is to-day assumed to prevail everywhere. In the earlier stages of the debate the map of the world drawn by science was only very partially filled in. It was like the old charts of Africa that some of us remember, with a thinly peopled coast-line; definite courses of rivers mapped up to a certain point inland, and then running out into dotted tracks, marking conjectures and inferences; mythical "Mountains of the Moon"—survivals from the old charts with their pictures of lions, and legends in crooked script, "Here there is much gold." There was a general idea of the prevalence throughout all the unmapped land of nature of a "reign of law." But the many gaps in the scientific account left room for both human and Divine freedom as well as "natural law." On the other hand it was believed that wherever science had given its account of any region, it gave the complete and final account of all that was in it, and the educated man's account of the world was thus a blend of the scientific and the religious interpretation, with elements from the latter filling in the gaps of the former, and with frontier controversies about the undetermined boundaries where the two interpretations seemed to conflict. Similar controversies occurred between Science and Art.

To this transition period belong these apologetic distinctions between Divine interventions and influencings of the "course of Nature" which were in accordance with the "reign of law" and those which were beyond it.

If we are to take it that from the scientific point of view, nature (*i.e.* the realm to which we have access through our senses) is a closed physical system, every event which takes place in the sensible world must be fully accounted for in terms of its physical antecedents, and brought within the causal nexus which it is the business of science to explore. Clearly, if this theory is to be taken as giving us a final and complete view of nature, there is no vital distinction between individual Providence, objective answers to prayer, and miracle. They are all in principle the same kind of thing. In each case something happens in nature that cannot be fully explained in terms of simple nature. There is in each of them something which implies that nature is not a closed system. The tightening-up of the idea of a general "reign of law" in Nature into the idea that Nature is a completely closed physical system has thus made this older apologetic obsolete.

Modernist theology has more or less recognised this, and has abandoned not only physical miracle but also that view of petitionary prayer which holds that it can influence the outward course of nature. It is dubious even about individual Providence. But it draws a deep distinction between the world of nature and the inner world of the soul. The real concern of science, it holds, is with physical nature. The real concern of religion is with the soul. Why then should we not definitely assign the physical realm wholly to science; reserving for religion the world of the spirit, the world of Divine and human freedom, of personal communion, the come and go of prayer and its answers, the region of struggle with temptation and victory by the aid of the Divine Spirit, the region, as Eucken asserts, of the new birth? Modernism is diverse and many-coloured and often rather hazy in its statements here. But this, I think, is its general drift if we are to take it from such exponents as Jowett and Martineau in last century and Harnack in this. Now we may fully admit that in its desire to meet science in this way Modernism was dealing with a real difficulty and was endeavouring to conserve a great human interest. For certainly the constancy of nature, of which the closed system theory is one expression, is one of the greatest human interests. The whole world of human society with all its ethical and religious possibilities depends upon our being able to count upon that regularity of natural process without which progress would be impossible. Yet, with all this, we must hold that the compromise which it has suggested and maintained is an impossible one, and is now definitely dated and in process of being transcended by the course of thought. It belongs to a certain definitely marked stage of scientific thought which it was designed to meet. At that period science was extraordinarily dogmatic and confident of her power to give a complete and final account of nature, to get deeper than philosophy, religion, or art in her account of reality. To-day, as we shall see, self-criticism has made her less sure of her powers in these ultimate regions.

In yet another way the situation has developed. Science has now passed definitely beyond the limits drawn by the Modernist compromise. She has, for a considerable time, been trying to fill up the blank spaces in her map of knowledge. She has carried her methods further and further afield into the psychological and sociological regions, and is endeavouring to bring them all within the causal nexus, and the reign of law. A reconciliation on the lines which the earlier Modernism suggested and which still linger in its later forms is therefore no longer possible.

A concordat which is definitely repudiated by one of the parties which it seeks to conciliate, has already become matter of past history. But, in truth, it was as unsatisfactory to religion as to science. The whole conception of physical nature as a closed system, if it be taken as an ultimate account, is, indeed, fatal to any really religious interpretation of life. The failure to understand this is the gravest error of the Modernist compromise.

Let us examine what are the inevitable consequences of treating the closed system idea of physical nature as axiomatic and final. First of all, it is quite impossible to reconcile it with human freedom. According to this view, the whole world of human action as distinct from human volition is part of the causal system of physical nature. Every action of man's physical organs, as well as every change in the tissues of his body and brain, all nerve processes, must necessarily be as truly physically determined as the movements of the clouds on the face of the heavens. They are completely accounted for when we have determined their place between their physical antecedents and consequents.

What, then, are we to make of the psychical life of man, his emotions, thoughts, and volitions? So far as man's bodily life is concerned, there is obviously nothing left for his psychical life to do, every action being already fully explained otherwise.

This was the great perplexity of the Victorian naturalism, which, in order to find some way out, invented the extraordinary theory of epiphenomenalism, which taught that the entire psychical life was a kind of ghostly accompaniment of physical processes without any influence on these processes themselves, like the shadows which accompany a train passing along a mountain-side, but which have no influence whatever on its traction. This theory was framed in large measure in order to meet the physicist's demands that the law of the conservation of energy should hold good for the body as a merely physical machine. But if the body was merely a physical machine, whence came the psychical life? It must either remain unexplained, or it must be physically caused. But if physical energy were expended in its production and maintenance, then the world could not be a closed system. It must leak energy at every pore of the human body. Space forbids further discussion of the theory. Dr Ward's annihilating criticism in his *Naturalism and Agnosticism* left little to be said of this crude first attempt to conserve the closed system and yet find a place for consciousness, thought, and volition.

It is impossible within the limits of this chapter to give even a summary of the various "parallelist" theories of body and mind which have endeavoured in a more thorough and plausible way to conserve the idea of nature as a closed physical system, while retaining a place for the autonomy of spirit. Modernism, in so far as it holds the closed system idea, must find its speculative basis in one or other of these. It is only possible here to give the common element in all the theories and to point out its fatal weakness at the critical point.

All parallelist theories hold that nature is a complete system which at no point is influenced by spirit or influences it. The two sets of processes, material and psychical, run parallel all the way, without interlocking at any point.

When expanded into a full speculative system and extended from the soul and body of man into a theory of the Universe, one aspect of which is supposed to be Nature and the other Spirit, with an underlying, unknown substance manifesting itself in both, parallelism has an imposing appearance and a prestige lent it by the great name of Spinoza. It is impossible adequately to discuss this most ambitious of the theories, but like all the rest, it has for all coherent Theists more than one fatal defect. All genuine Theism demands that we shall look upon the Universe as a purposive system, directed towards the creation of free human souls. These souls are by the Theistic view made in God's image and capable of communion with Him. They are, like their Maker, free purposive agents, made to seek Truth, Beauty, and Goodness. Now, how can such free autonomous human life correspond point for point with a rigorously determined causal chain of physical processes? It is a sheer impossibility. Further, it would seem to follow that if man's psychical life runs rigorously parallel with its bodily counterpart, it must necessarily pass out of existence when the body dies and is resolved into its elements. Such are the insuperable difficulties which lie in wait for every Theist who plays with parallelism. There are many other equally unanswerable problems lying in wait for philosophy. Finally common sense rebels against the idea that the pleasures and pains which we experience have no influence whatever upon our bodily actions, that the volition which I make to raise my hand has no influence whatever upon the bodily action, and so on.

But these general absurdities must be left to the writers who have so thoroughly discussed the whole subject. The parallelist theory in all its forms, like epiphenomenalism, is in fact a highly artificial theory invented to find a thinkable way out of a real difficulty. That difficulty is the direct consequence of the closed system dogma and the unworkableness of all the epiphenomenalist and parallelist theories is, in fact, a *reductio ad absurdum* of the theory that physical nature is a closed system. When any theory leads men to intolerably cumbrous and artificial consequences, the human mind retrieves the balance by examining its presuppositions. If it finds that any of these are questionable, it makes a fresh beginning.

This is the stage which progressive religious and scientific thought seems now to have reached, and with it to be passing away at once from the hard and fast scientific dogmatism of last century, and also from that premature attempt to effect a concordat which we have called Modernism.

In a series of striking chapters in his recent volume on *Science and the Modern World*, Professor Whitehead has shown how the growth of the mechanical scheme of science, based on the physics of Newton and the chemistry of Dalton, troubled and confused the whole higher life and thought of the nineteenth century. The scheme worked so well in the region of physical discovery and technical mastery of nature, that men thought that they had penetrated to the very heart of the Universe, and laid their hands on absolute Reality. That reality behind all the glory of nature and all the *Divina Commedia* of human life was a world of round, hard atoms like billiard balls, gyrating in space according to certain discoverable uniformities. This was the objective truth, and all that the poets and painters and saints and prophets could tell us belonged to a purely human and subjective world. I remember once seeing a carefully painted picture of a human skull, with the grim title, " Behind the Mask." It was symbolic of the prevalent mechanistic view of the Universe of the mid-Victorian time. Behind the living and breathing earth and world of humanity men had discovered as the last reality the gaunt skeleton of Matter and Energy, or as Spencer said, " the Force from which all things proceed." To-day we have passed into a different world. It is not too much to say that the youngest and freshest thought of science itself discerns that the gaunt skeleton disclosed by the physical sciences is itself a mask of something or Some One deeper still, in other words, that in itself science can only give us an aspect of reality.

Many factors have contributed to this conclusion. The world of values has asserted itself. No system of cosmic interpretation that is in fundamental strife with the highest intuitions of the artist and the prophet can permanently hold the mind of man.

Moreover, the mere growth of scientific knowledge, the new developments in physics, and in particular the expansion of biology and psychology have strained the mechanistic theory, under which science has achieved many victories in other spheres of inquiry, beyond the breaking-point. The present condition of chemistry for instance has been compared to that of the Ptolemaic theory of astronomy, which became so complicated and difficult by the mere growth of knowledge and the framing of subsidiary hypotheses to restore its validity, that the simpler Copernican theory had an easy triumph.

Finally, we may fairly claim that the mere advance of Epistemology has given the final blow to the dogmatic tyranny of the mechanistic Victorian science. Yet it was with a view to conciliate this now weakened dogmatism that the Modernist concordat with its rejection of miracle, of special Providence, and of outward answers to prayer came into being, and it bears therefore on its very face the marks of this vanishing order of thought. It is as clear as daylight that we must reconsider the whole position relative to miracle not only in the light of the whole Christian doctrine of the world, of which it was from the first a part, but in the light of that fascinating but as yet inchoate world of new scientific outlook which is coming into being.

But, to return, it is necessary to reiterate that what religion has to think of first is not the specific question of the miraculous, but the much larger question of the Christian doctrine of the world, of which the other is only a part.

With that doctrine we cannot realise too clearly that the dogma of the closed system of nature is in diametrical opposition. Both cannot be true. Now, in what way does the modern movement in science and in philosophy ease the tension of the whole situation, and open up the way for final reconciliation ?

It is, of course, impossible here to give anything but a bare summary of the difference between the scientific outlook half a century ago and to-day, as it presents itself to one who is interested mainly in the epistemological side of science, and has no claim to be anything but an outsider in the realm of science itself.

In the closing years of the Victorian period the dispassionate scientific outlook was contrasted by many of its supporters with the religious outlook, which was simply the pathetic illusion created by man's hopes. God, said Feuerbach, was the projection on the heavens of man's own shadow, the Brocken phantom of his desires. To base one's beliefs on one's emotional needs, said Huxley, was "immoral." Over against this interested view of the Universe stood the absolutely disinterested, final, and demonstrated interpretation of science. We have the same contrast asserted to-day by the Marxian materialism. Scientific knowledge gives us reality. Religion is "dope," the opiate invented for the proletariat by capitalism.

The poets mirrored the difficult position.

Tennyson, in *In Memoriam*, elected for faith, but obviously was gravely troubled by the supposed conflict with "freezing reason."

> "Like a man in wrath the heart
> Stood up, and answered, 'I have felt.'"

In the last issue he accepted the position that religion was a matter of feeling, but asserted its rights none the less as based somehow on true knowledge.

Matthew Arnold elected for doubt—

"Nor does the being hungry prove that we have bread."

To-day we can give a much more adequate vindication of faith as the highest reason, and on the other hand the whole scientific method has been exposed to rigorous analysis by some of its own leading exponents. The general result of that analysis has been that, far from being an absolutely disinterested instrument, the scientific method is much liker a calculus than a philosophy. In its formation, and in the formation of ordinary common-sense knowledge, of which it is only a more fully developed form, two practical aims have all along been prominent, the description and the forecasting of phenomena.

Man finds himself in the heart of a vast phantasmagoria of sense phenomena of infinite variety and complexity. He has the will to live, but he very soon discovers that in order to live he must do something much more than stand passively contemplating the great sense-pageant which is continually sweeping over and around and beneath him. He must in some way devise means to ward off those painful and destroying phenomena which we call hunger, disease, pain, and, above all, that termination of his experience which we call death. He must for this end be able to share his experiences and thoughts with others, in other words to describe them; and together they must also learn to forecast what is coming next in the great phantasmagoria, and make provision for it. Out of these two necessities, description and forecast, arises our ordinary conceptual "common-sense" knowledge, and the scientific view of things which is only a greatly refined and developed form of the other. To this latter we shall in the main confine ourselves, as the greater includes the less.

There are three outstanding methods of scientific knowledge by which these practical ends of description and forecast are attained—classification, analysis, and the discovery of uniform processes, analogically called "laws."[1]

(1) *Classification.*—The human mind would be absolutely overpowered and paralysed by the multitude and variety of the phenomena which are continually appearing and disappearing, and it would be utterly unable to have any social life or community of thought with others unless it had invented the process of classifying and conceptualising. An infinite Intelligence would have no need of any such device as conceptual thinking. It springs from man's finitude, but none the less it is an immense advance upon mere instinct and automatic reaction. By it man is able to form concepts and common terms. He groups certain things or persons together, by observing similarities and ignoring differences, and he arranges the whole under common terms, so that he can talk rationally about them with his fellows. Conceptual thinking thus marks man's advance beyond the animal, the instinctive, and the automatic.

Scientific classification is a great extension of this

[1] See Canon Streeter's volume on *Reality*, chapter iv. to which in this section I am indebted for frequent clearing of my own thoughts.

method. Every new science must necessarily begin with this ordering and arrangement of its data, by this device of finite thought. Its purpose is defined by Mill (*Logic*, book iv., chap. vii., section 1) as follows: "to secure that things shall be thought of in such groups, and those groups in such an order, as will best conduce to the remembrance and the ascertainment of their laws."

Now it is quite clear that this can only be done by ignoring certain differences and by emphasising similarities in the phenomena classified together—*i.e.* by a certain suppression of what is really there. At the bottom of the scale of existences, in the purely physical region, where there is far more resemblance between the objects classified than there is higher up the ladder, this may not matter much, but the higher up the scale of being we go, the more does individuality count. There is, for instance, a far greater difference between one animal and another than there is between two molecules of a material substance, and *a fortiori* there is incomparably more difference between one human being and another.

We have here, it is clear, a grave limitation of the purely inductive method which inheres in its very nature, the inability of a method which is continually in quest of general truths and laws to deal with individuality.

Why is it that any one of us would feel insulted if he were told that he must think so and so, or act in a certain way because he belonged to a certain nationality or social class? Is it not because we feel that the offender is deliberately ignoring our individuality ? Yet in doing so, he is following the inductive method of classification. Be it noted, that the defect inheres in the method as such. The failure in any case lies not in bad classification, nor in an incomplete classification. It lies in the fact that, as regards the point at issue, there is a classification at all. Every rational human being knows that, for good or ill, he is not quite the same as any of his fellows. We seem, then, to have discovered at the very roots of the inductive method clear indication of the impossibility of science giving us a final and complete account of any man.

(2) We pass on to another essential of scientific method, *Analysis*. Still pursuing its quest for the power to describe and forecast phenomena, science follows the method of analysis. This is as essential a part of its method as the synthetic process of classification. An apparently simple phenomenon baffles it in its quest for a law. But it lays siege to it and shows that it is made up of parts, and then is able to bring the parts under the law. So science has worked its way back from the molecule to the atom, and from the atom to the electron. Whether it will stop there, who can say ?

Now it is often possible to divide inorganic things without getting away from reality. We can usually assemble the parts again. But we cannot do that with living things without losing something irreparable. Wordsworth felt that of the living world of nature, and, as Professor Whitehead has shown, was deeply at odds with the scientific spirit of his time, and put his indictment in a pungent line, " We murder to dissect." That is to say, when we try to dissolve a living thing into parts, its essence disappears. So is it always with individuality, as the very name should show us. It cannot be divided. So it eludes both classification and analysis. It cannot be completely divided any more than it can be generalised. Whatever pathological states of a human being may alternate in the field of a human consciousness so that a man thinks himself " legion," as in the Gospels, or as in the well-known instance of " divided personality " recounted by Dr Morton Prince, the personality is never really divided into other personalities. No sane observer of either case partook of the same illusion as did the patient. You cannot really divide a personality without annihilating it.

(3) *Law*.—Finally, the ultimate aim of all science is to forecast the future and so to win control over nature. It seeks the power of prevision with a view to provision. Its aim is therefore to discover uniformities or " laws " in nature such that, when we can bring any one phenomenon under them, we shall be able to count on its recurrence and prepare for what is coming next. These uniformities by analogy with human society are called " laws " of nature. The sovereign importance of this orderliness in nature, indeed its absolute practical necessity for human life and for the very existence and growth of all forms of rational society, is clear. If the same food sometimes poisoned and sometimes nourished life, if fire did not always warm, if harvest did not result from sowing, in a word, if nature were capricious instead of orderly, how impossible civilised existence would be! Science is

thus always seeking for laws of phenomena, and when it has found and formulated them, it is always seeking to bring new facts under them, by classification and analysis, and so to be able to predict or cause the succession of these facts in the future.

Another way of putting the same thing is to say that science is always seeking for causes. It has long been shown that so far as strict science is concerned, this means simply uniform sequences. Cause is a metaphysical idea.

Now the more we study all the forms of the inductive arguments, the more clear does it become that every one of them and the whole process of induction rests for its validity upon one great conviction, the belief in the Uniformity of Nature. In all induction we start out from the conviction that, however disordered and mixed up the processes of nature may appear, they are in reality all ordered, and in all our classifying, observing, and analysing, our persistent motive is to discover that order.

The strength of this fundamental conviction is forcibly brought out by Sigwart in his great treatise on *Logic*.[2] "However we may fail in our attempts to subordinate the world of perception to a complete conceptual system and to deduce all events from universally valid laws, we never doubt the truth of our principles. We still maintain that even the worst confusion is capable of being resolved into comprehensible formulæ; again and again we start our work anew and believe—not that nature opposed an inexorable refusal to our endeavours—

[2] Vol. ii. p. 17, E.T.

but only that as yet we have failed to find the right way; but this perseverance is due to the conviction that we ought not to despair of the accomplishment of our task, and the energy of the explorer is sustained by the obligatory force of a moral idea."

Now what is the origin of this rooted conviction that, however chaotic she may appear, Nature is really orderly, which makes us assume this and stick to it in spite of constant frustration ? To point to the advance of science and the gradual discovery of order in those parts of Nature where the hypothesis of uniformity has been put to the test, and to argue that therefore the same uniformity will be found everywhere else, is to beg the whole question. We can show no sufficient logical reason at all for our faith in the universal uniformity of nature. Who can tell but that beyond the relatively small mapped-out region we may at any moment come upon tracts of pure chaos ? Why in all the laboratories and observatories of the world are thousands of investigators still going on attacking that chaos sustained by that brave and perisistent faith of which Sigwart speaks ?

It is a truly wonderful spectacle, and it becomes not the less but the more wonderful when we realise the fact on which I think logicians are now generally agreed,[3] that this great sustaining condition

[3] Professor Whitehead has recently made the interesting suggestion that in Europe we owe the peculiar intensity of this confidence in the rationality of nature out of which science has sprung to the mediæval schooling in the rationality of God. This is probably true, but I believe the roots lie deeper in universal common-sense knowledge.—*Science and the Modern World*, pp. 14, 15.

is in truth a postulate, that we owe it to the will, and to a certain deep and vital faith that nature is on the side of all that man counts most dear in his earthly life. Have we not here that same primitive "trustfulness" which, as Dr Ward has said, leads all living things to make adventures, and has impelled them to advance from the waters to the land and from the land to the air?

But assuredly the assumption that the whole vast natural Universe must be orderly is seen to be an adventure of singular audacity when we think of the tiny little "home-farm of Earth," which is our abode, and the enormous Universe of which it is an infinitesimal fraction.

But if such be the nature of the very foundations of science, it will clearly not do for us to claim for its account of the Universe that complete disinterestedness and finality which the Victorian scientific age claimed for it, or to treat it as more than one way among others of conceiving and of handling the world. The marvellous success of the postulate indeed shows that there must be something in the very construction of nature, so far as we know her, friendly to human interests and akin to human thought, something deeply encouraging to those who desire to make further assumptions of faith in the moral purpose of the Universe. But in the light of the disclosure of the real nature of the postulate which underlies all scientific thought, it does not lie with science to arrogate to itself the claim to be more than a successful method of describing and forecasting the processes of nature. Does it carry us further? Can we say that it can completely explore and describe and forecast " the abysmal deeps of personality " ? That it has been endeavouring to extend our knowledge of that microcosm within the macrocosm, we know. But of psychology, both old and new, we can say two things. First of all, like biology, only in a greater degree, inasmuch as it too is concerned with general concepts and laws, it can never fully explain any human being. Laws can only deal with uniformities of action. They are, indeed, as has been said, simply uniformities formulated in order that we may bring new facts under them for description and for forecast.

Now let us take our most intimate friend and try to describe him in terms of all that physics, chemistry, biology, anthropology, psychology, and sociology can do. As we build up our portentous description of abstractions, we may recognise that each particular specification contributed by all the relevant sciences is true, and when we add them all together they may enrich to a large extent our knowledge of him. They are all true, so far as they go, but can any human being say that this complex of abstractions is the very man ? Something vital and momentous has slipped through all the meshes of all the nets. Something, it is true, remains ; something which he has in common with a multitude of other men, but the man himself is not there ! The description has failed. This is verified when, in the second place, we turn from description to forecast. Has science succeeded here ? We all know that science has done nothing of the kind, that all our knowledge of all the relevant sciences cannot enable us definitely to predict what any waking and rational human individual will be thinking, saying, or doing in an hour, still less a month, and still less a year from now. This is the more remarkable when we think of the astonishing accuracy of scientific precision in physical matters. You can tell with absolute certainty what a planet will do, but what transit instrument will reveal the journey of a man?

Now there are still highly intelligent people who cherish the idea that this admitted uncertainty as to what human beings will do or become is due to the fact that as yet we do not know all the laws of psychology.

Herbert Spencer compared this uncertainty to the uncertainty we have as to the precise pathways that will be taken by the fragments of a bursting shell. We can tell where the shell will fall, but we cannot beforehand locate the shards. The uncertainty in the latter case, he said, is plainly due simply to our own ignorance of many facts about the explosive and the shell. But if we knew these, as we can learn to know them, we would be able to locate each pathway to a certainty. So is it with human beings. If we push on with the various sciences involved, we shall in time be able to forecast human action as accurately as planetary movement. Do not insurance tables imply that we know what men in the mass will do? Push the method further and you will be able to forecast everything that the individual will do, also.

This is a mere dream. The same reason which prevents the scientific description of your friend ever being anything but a cumbrous and lifeless model of him, will absolutely preclude all the scientific knowledge of him which you can acquire from enabling you completely to forecast his actions and thoughts. The reason of this is, as I have said, that in the very nature of the case no abstract scientific description can ever give you the individuality of the man, and without knowing that you cannot predict what he will do.

But, it may be said, I am not so ignorant as all that of what my friend is, and to a certain extent, of what he will do. I have a knowledge of him other than that cumbrous scientific model, and I do know his character, so that, barring my uncertainties as to the environments in which he may be placed, which uncertainty is largely due to my (removable) ignorance, I can tell, generally, how he will respond to them. I know his individuality and his character, and these give me confidence.

That is, of course, perfectly true. But the essential point is that you do not have that individual knowledge through science. It comes to you in quite a different way, through what Bergson calls intuition. We know our own personalities not through generalising about them but by immediate knowledge, and through that knowledge we have the clue to other personalities, and are enabled thereby to interpret their actions and characters and truly to know them as individuals like ourselves, though so unique a thing is individuality that even with this new source of knowledge we can never exhaustively fathom or truly, definitely, and completely forecast the action of even our most intimate friend.

To sum up the argument, science has wonderfully extended the range of human knowledge. By its means we have immensely developed our power of describing and of forecasting and controlling nature, and secured so great an increase of comprehension, and of enjoyment of life, that men have been led gravely to exaggerate its possibilities. But in its very nature it is subject to certain uncertainties and limitations. It cannot give us final truth about anything, and by its very nature, also, it cannot explain so great a reality in human experience and in the higher range of nature as individuality. Yet individuality is unquestionably there functioning in all living things, and above all in human life, reacting on the living body, and through it upon the spatial and ponderable world of nature.

It is as certain that we act as that we are. Personality certainly functions in the nature world. We do not simply contemplate, we influence or change nature. I can move my body and alter the physical dispositions of the objects around me, and my individuality counts in this. But if that be so, clearly, then nature is not a completely closed system. It is to a certain extent plastic to the influence of my personal volitions. Either this is true, or, to reason back, science can completely explain personality, and in that case each of us can be completely described in strictly general terms, can be wholly subsumed under universal laws, and in spite of the clamant witness of language the individual can be divided. Dissection can in a word be done without murder. We can completely describe each man without going beyond what is common to him and other men, and sooner or later we shall be able to predict what any man will do at any moment as accurately as a transit instrument can track the path of a planet. On such a view, of course, freedom vanishes. Either we must face these incredible consequences or we must abandon the idea that physical nature is a closed system, and must admit that up to a certain point she is plastic in the hands of man, because she does what cannot be fully explained in terms of physical law.

This, I take it, is what Lord Kelvin had before him when he wrote the much canvassed opinion that from the point of view of science every free human action was a miracle. He meant that voluntary human action is inexplicable in scientific terms.

We pass here a step beyond saying that science can only deal with an aspect of reality, a truth which might be held by a parallelist, to a further statement of its essential limitations. Pure science cannot give us a complete account even of what goes on in what we know as the material world, as, for instance, my bodily actions. There are and must be events in the physical realm which cannot be exhaustively described in terms of physical causation, events which are fully historic, but of which science can never give an account. I see nothing in the methods of inductive logic to preclude this. If the uniformity of Nature be a simple postulate, and if the inductive methods be, as I believe they are, " a net to catch certain kinds of fish, and to let other fish through," there is no antecedent obstacle to such a position. Among these escaping fish that argument would compel us to put many of man's physical actions and achievements in the physical regions. They do not contravene the natural laws, they simply elude them. They cannot be described fully by science, and, as we should expect, they cannot be accurately predicted by science. To this elusion of biological science by much of the realm of human action we may find a significant analogy in biology itself. Dr Haldane in his Gifford lectures, which are being delivered while these words are being written, finds himself compelled to discard both the mechanical and the vitalist theories of life. He is clear that the characteristics of living things cannot be fully accounted for in terms of physical and chemical mechanism. Yet, with the great majority of biologists, he discards the conception of a special vital force interposing to overrule chemical processes as too crude to account for the phenomena of life. How does he meet the situation? He supposes that the physical and chemical sciences do not give a complete account even of their own inorganic domain. Something is present even there that eludes their nets. We can at present give no adequate account of what it is. But when living things appear it manifests itself in their peculiar characteristics. It has escaped the meshes of the nets of the physicist and chemist, but it is detected by the biologist. Have we any reason to suppose that the nets of the biologist have captured everything that there is in man? If there is something in man that stubbornly refuses to be described in purely biological terms and that cannot be predicted, have we not precisely the same right as the biologist has, as in the other case, to say that even his marvellous science cannot say the final word about humanity? We can, I believe, as has been said, go further still and say that no inductive science, not even psychology and sociology themselves, can ever give us an exhaustive account of human history.

Now if this reasoning has been sound, we must abandon the idea that it is any necessary dogma of science that nature is in itself a rigid system, impervious and inflexible to the spiritual world.

We shall see in Chapter V how the whole dogma originated from a very natural fallacy of reasoning. Meantime it is enough to say that it leads not only to other impossible conclusions, but that it fails to take any adequate account of individuality and the difference which individuality makes in nature. Finally we have seen that the real nature we know is to a great extent plastic to the influences exerted upon it by the free human spirit. Man can be a providence to his children within that realm of nature, he can hear and answer their prayers; and if Lord Kelvin was right, he can produce effects in nature which from the point of view of science are miracles. We press the question —If these things are possible to man, are they impossible to God? If He be the Almighty Father of Humanity, are they even unlikely?

It is along these lines, opened up by the development of scientific logic itself, and not imposed upon it by the demands of theology, that there lies the real prospect of a definite and final reconciliation between the abstract and general view of science and the "personal and romantic" view of religion, between the view which holds that the world of nature is rigid, and that it is plastic in the hands of God. The necessity for supposing it rigid arises only when we insist that the scientific view gives a complete and final account of nature. When this is abandoned there is room for the poet, room for the moralist, and room for the whole religious interpretation of the world. There remains in a word no reason why both the scientific and religious views of the world should not be true. The scientific view corresponds to the Registrar-General's returns—so many births, deaths, marriages and so forth in the year. All such details are indispensable for a country's political, economic, and hygienic life. But over and above these how much there is that only the historian, the novelist, the poet, or the musician can teach us! Is that all? Surely the last and deepest word of all lies with the man of faith, who lives by listening for the Divine Voice and reaching out for the Divine Hand.

But if it be so the whole Modernist repudiation of the miracles of Jesus loses its real intellectual basis.

These unique deeds are seen to be the natural results within a Spiritual Universe of the appearance of a unique Personality. But they are unique in degree, not in kind.

CHAPTER V

NATURE AND MORALITY

At the beginning of this volume we called attention to the singular paradox that whereas, in the first age of Christianity the miracles of Jesus were regarded as glories of the faith, which the Church up to its powers sought to imitate, as charismata or graces of the Spirit, to-day they are regarded by many as among its chief difficulties. In the historical review there given I have sought to show how the change came about, by the gradual rise of the conception of the Reign of Law in nature, which has to-day developed into the further idea that physical nature is a completely self-enclosed system of physical causes and effects.

The practical adoption of this idea from contemporary science by much current idealism and also current Modernist theology has led many to identify the "laws of Nature" with the laws of God, and under the influence of this confusion to confine the sphere of petitionary prayer to purely spiritual matters, and to rule out the whole conception of "miracle" as obsolete, inasmuch as it was supposed to imply an interference by God with His own laws. In the last chapter we have seen how partial and belated this concept of Nature has become, and how necessary it has also become for Modernist thinkers to reconsider their over-hasty concession to the supposed necessities of science.

But there is still another cause of the extraordinary revolution of which I have spoken. Modernist religious thought, under the influence of science and philosophical idealism, has moved away from the fundamental Biblical idea of the deep and vital connection between man's sins and the outward evils of this life, the tragic element in human experience, famine, disease, and premature death.

The contrast between the prevailing thought of our day and that of the Old Testament and the first Christian age is that whereas the modern mind is perfectly willing to admit and enforce the connection between ignorance and death, it is wholly scornful of there being any relation whatever between sin and death. Hence that which gave their chief meaning and glory to the "signs" of Jesus and to His Resurrection has been wellnigh lost by the men of to-day. Their very defenders have forgotten to defend them on this ground, and regard them merely as signs of Divine power, and the last thing the apologists of to-day think of is precisely the thing which made them so attractive to the apologists of the first age. To these they were the supreme signs that the tragic powers of both sin and death were broken, and the true idea of the Divine Creator was at last being visibly realised, and would be completed even in this suffering, sorrowing, and dying world of men. To them the miracles of Jesus were "signs" of the coming of heaven to earth, anticipation of the triumph of spirit, as the charm of the first spring flowers is that they are the heralds of all the glories of coming summer.

From these two causes, the rise of the idea of a rigid natural order and the weakening of the idea of a moral order in the world of nature, it has come about that what to the first Christian age were manifestations, are to us interruptions of the Divine Order. We have transferred our conception of the Divine Order from the moral to the physical region.

We have now, therefore, fairly to face the question whether this fundamental idea of the Bible that sin leads inevitably not only to moral and spiritual decay but to outward tragedy and physical calamity of all kinds, is obsolete, or whether it is and must ever be a living and formidable part of the Christian interpretation of life. Is it, or is it not, true that "sin" leads to "death"?

The question to-day is closed for many because they think it is inseparably associated with the story of Eden—the coming of death into the human world and Adam's sin. The real question has little or nothing to do with the myth. Every real student of the Bible knows that the principle that sin always works on toward death and woe goes through it all from beginning to end. The myth, as Dr Denney has said, was created by the faith, not the faith by the myth. The faith as distinct from the myth grew out of the Hebrew idea of God as an ethical being, and is, as I hope to show, still inseparable from any fully thought-out Theism.

Why is the faith for the moment in an eclipse which throws several of the vital ideas of Christianity as it were, out of focus, depriving them of half their meaning and power? I do not know any one who has put the matter so incisively as Dr Denney.

"Probably the most widespread idea," he writes, "about the relation of the natural to the spiritual world is that which simply contrasts them. They are realities which stand apart, which do not interpenetrate, which are simply neutral to each other. At the utmost, nature is that stage on which the moral life is transacted. But it is quite indifferent to the quality of that life. The laws of nature are the same for the good man as for the bad: the flood drowns them both, and the lightning does not go out of the way of either. It is even argued that this moral neutrality of nature is necessary to protect the integrity of the moral life. If nature immediately sided with virtue and opposed vice, if she did justice on her stage at every turn, disinterested goodness would be impossible: men would never be able to prove that they loved goodness for its own sake. Without disputing the amount of truth that there is in this view, it is apparent that it is not adequate to the depth and subtlety of the facts. Nature is not merely the stage of the moral life, but in some sense its soil. The moral life is not merely transacted in the face of nature: it is rooted in it, and grows up in profound and vital relations to it. The nature which is absolutely severed from the spiritual life —which does nothing but confront it in serene or scornful impartiality—is not the real nature in which we live and move and have our being. It is one of the abstractions which physical science constructs for its own convenience, but which are apt to mislead rather than enlighten in philosophy or theology. The only real nature is that to which we and our spiritual experiences are vitally related, and our problem is not to acquiesce in the idea of the ethical neutrality of nature . . . but to see in it, in the last result, the manifestation, the organ, the ally of God. The universe is a system of things in which good can be planted, and in which it can bear fruit; it is also a system of things in which there is a ceaseless and unrelenting reaction against evil. This view of nature is vital both to the doctrine of sin and to that of reconciliation."[1] I would add to this last sentence that it is vital also to faith in the Divine Providence, and in the power of prayer to influence natural events, as also to the understanding of the "miracles" of the New Testament in particular, and, above all, those of our Lord.

In the above passage Dr Denney points out that the thinking of the modern mind with which he is dealing has its origin in the scientific method of dealing abstractly with all its problems. It views each field in which for the moment it is working, *e.g.*, physics, chemistry, and biology, in abstraction from other areas—*i.e.*, as if it were a separate and complete field of knowledge. It assumes, as a working postulate, the independence of its own field. As a matter of fact, all the areas

[1] *The Christian Doctrine of Reconciliation*, pp. 201, 202.

are interconnected in the great web of nature, and interact with each other. But the investigator gets to work as if it were not so. Now what is perfectly admissible as a working method leads to the gravest errors, if we forget the "let it be granted" with which we started and exalt the postulate into a dogma. This is precisely what has happened with the inclusive abstraction of "Nature," which science has framed to describe the total world of sense phenomena. Nature in this sense is in fact only a part of a much larger whole, the total world of the Universe, with which it is in interrelation and interaction. It is in this abstraction and in its evolution into a dogma that we find the roots of that fallacy of the "closed system" idea of nature, and of nature's moral neutrality which has caused such mischievous and widespread confusion in the period of thought from which we are now emerging. What confusion and distress it has caused since the days of Mill's famous outburst on the crimes of "Nature" let one or two often-quoted passages bear witness. In the most remarkable of all his essays, the Romanes Lecture of 1893, Huxley, to the dismay of his fellow-evolutionists, impeached the Cosmic process in language almost as vehement as that of Mill. "The Cosmic process" (*i.e.*, "Nature") encourages "ruthless self-assertion," the "thrusting aside of all competitors," and teaches the "gladiatorial theory of existence. It has no sort of relation to moral ends." "The imitation of it by man is inconsistent with the first principles of ethics." The conclusion is inevitable: "Let us understand, once for all, that the ethical progress of Society depends not on imitating the Cosmic process, still less in running away from it, but in combating it." A decade or two later Mr Bertrand Russell, in one of his chameleon phases of philosophic outlook, gives equally passionate expression to his sense of man's pitiful case in the presence of an almighty and indifferent Nature. He is impressed by the appalling contrast between man's moral ideals of justice, mercy, and truth, and the brutal world of reality in which man finds himself imprisoned. He is perfectly certain that there is nothing to be said for a God over both. In such dismaying conditions what can a free man do to keep his soul alive? How in such an alien and inhuman world can so powerless a creature as man preserve his aspirations untarnished? "A strange mystery it is that Nature, omnipotent but blind, in the revolutions of her secular hurryings through the abysses of space, has brought forth at last a child, subject still to her power, but gifted with sight, with knowledge of good and evil, with the capacity of judging all the works of his unthinking Mother. In spite of Death, the mark and seal of the parental control, Man is yet free during his brief years to examine, to criticise, to know, and in imagination—to execute. To him alone in the world with which he is acquainted, this belongs; and in this lies his superiority to the resistless forces that control his natural life." A fierce passage follows in which Mr Russell condemns mere acquiescence in and flattery of the ways of Nature. "The religion of Moloch—as such creeds may be generically called—is in essence the cringing submission of the slave who does not love in his heart. Since the independence of ideals is not yet acknowledged, Power may be freely worshipped, and receive an unlimited respect despite its wanton infliction of pain. When we have realised that Power is largely bad, that man, with his knowledge of good and evil, is but a helpless atom in a world which has no such knowledge, the choice is again presented to us. Shall we worship Force or shall we worship Goodness? Shall our God resist the evil or shall He be recognised as the creation of our own goodness?"[2]

In citing these indictments of Mill, Huxley, and Russell, we have certainly travelled a long way from Wordsworth.

> Nature never did betray
> The heart that loved her; 'tis her privilege
> Through all the years of this our life to lead
> From joy to joy: for she can so inform
> The mind that is within us, so impress
> With quietness and beauty and so feed
> With lofty thoughts, that neither evil tongues,
> Rash judgments nor the sneers of selfish men
> Nor greetings, where no kindness is, nor all
> The dreary intercourse of daily life
> Shall e'er prevail against us, or disturb
> Our cheerful faith that all which we behold
> Is full of blessings. Therefore let the noon
> Shine on thee in thy solitary walk,
> And let the misty mountain winds be free
> To blow against thee.

---

[2] Phil. Essays, *A Free Man's Worship*, pp. 66-68, ed. 1910.

There is something more here than mere contrast, there is downright contradiction. We are filled with sheer bewilderment. How can ordinary intelligent men, and still more, how can men of uncommon mental distinction take such glaringly opposite views of Nature? It is hardly too much to say that while to the poet Nature, in her relations with men, is a Divinity, to the men of science quoted she is, except that they look on her as unconscious, a kind of devil. We can only really account for so singular a contradiction when we realise that they mean different things by the same term, Nature. In Wordsworth we have the religious view of Nature, which is synoptic in character, Nature as part of a great whole in which God is working out supreme ethical and spiritual ends. The assurance as to this enables him, unlike these others, to feel that he is not living in an alien but in a friendly world, and in the beauty of Nature to find a sacrament and a benediction.

The Nature which the others are thinking of is a Nature which for purposes of scientific investigation has been severed from its context in the whole, severed on one side from God and on the other from man, and assumed to be uninfluenced by, and unconscious of, either. In other words, we have an "idol" of the study and the laboratory, created by a logical blunder, substituted for the Nature that we used to know. The perplexity and trouble caused by this to men, who have to a large extent retained the Christian moral values, is sufficiently obvious to all sympathetic readers of these three remarkable essays.

We have in the past century had all kinds of attempted reconstructions of belief based on the attempt to combine what was felt to be most precious in the moral and spiritual inheritance of the past with this supposed intellectual necessity, that Nature should be regarded as a closed physical system, closed, in effect, from both God and man, indifferent to moral and spiritual distinctions, bent only on maintaining the uniformity of her own working. The idea, as we have seen, had an almost hypnotic influence on the great Victorians. They were not always in the same mind as the essayists of whom I have spoken. Sometimes they made the best of it, and found something glorious in the serene neutrality of Nature, and desired it for themselves rather than the feverish action and passions of men.

> From the intense clear star-sown vault of heaven,
> Over the lit sea's unquiet way,
> In the rustling night air came the answer,
> Wouldst thou be as these are, live as they ?
>
> And with joy the stars perform their shining,
> And the sea its long moon-silvered roll,
> For, self-poised they live nor pine with noting
> All the fever of some differing soul.
>
> Bounded by themselves and unregardful
> In what state God's other works may be,
> In their own tasks all their powers outpouring,
> These attain the mighty life you see.

So sang Matthew Arnold. How he reconciled it with his faith that over the neutrality of Nature was " a Power not ourselves that makes for righteousness," I do not know that he ever explained. But there were various other attempts at synthesis. I think that probably most Victorian Modernists who gave serious and educated thought to the problem so poignantly put by Huxley in the Romanes Lecture, and who saw the impossibility of his view that mere "Nature" could produce a being higher than herself, and accepted therefore some Theistic or at least idealistic view of the Universe, effected their synthesis in some such way as this.

"Nature," in effect they said, "is a self-enclosed, neutral system. It is God's instrument for creating and disciplining souls. It may have other purposes, but this is the one that most clearly reveals its Creator's purpose, for His nature is most plainly manifest in man's ideals. But in order to be His instrument or tool, Nature must be herself. Just as a weapon or tool of man must first be itself, if it is to be of any use to him, must have its constant weight, shape, and edge, so Nature must have her own determinate constant properties and laws of operation. To observe these is her one concern, as God's servant. He will do the rest in the making of souls." Here we have a really serious attempt at synthesis, though I doubt if the last sentence is any longer relevant, since science has thrown the network of the causal judgment beyond what used to be called Nature, into the psychological and sociological realm, and refuses to recognise that there is any region into which she cannot come and completely explain. If the purely scientific view be a complete and final view, there seems to be nothing left for God to do, and the scientific account must completely displace the religious interpretation.

But independently of this, is this synthesis of God, a closed and morally neutral system of Nature and man, really a complete and satisfactory account of the processes of Nature and history ?

First of all, it is obviously Deistic in its form. We seem back in the position which Carlyle satirised, "An absentee God sitting outside His world, watching it go ! "

There is surely something defective, something savouring fatally of the mechanistic idea of nature, in the middle term of the three—which we have borrowed from the laboratory of science, to fit into a triad of which the other two members are derived from other regions, religious faith and personal intuition. Has not God put something of Himself into Nature, then, and still more into man, other than science can give any account of ? If so, Nature is more than a tool, and man more than an external product.

But without departing from the closed system idea of Nature, we may, perhaps, get a better simile to describe her than a tool. Nature is like a great factory, which for its smooth and efficient running needs to have its hard and fast laws for all its operatives, even though they be members of the owner's own family. And we may even think of it as a factory designed not only to turn out carpets or hardware, but to train manufacturers on a smaller scale ! But the more we humanise the illustration, the more, that is to say, we get down to realities, the more we shall be in danger of departing from the closed system idea altogether. It becomes impossible to think of such a factory system as being ever in absolute moral neutrality to the conduct of the family under training. The illustration, as we try to bring it more into agreement with plain facts, breaks down in our hands.

But it is time now to raise the question that has been lurking in the background all along. Is it really true to the facts to say that the great system of Nature, as we know it, is absolutely indifferent to the moral character and conduct of the men and women who live within it? Is it true, as Huxley and Russell, in their passionate revolt against the tyranny of the Nature in which they believe, seem sometimes to say, that Nature is actually hostile to man's highest ideals? If the picture which these draw of the "cosmic order" and "Nature" be literally true, then the whole religious interpretation of Nature must, of course, go by the board, as well as all idealistic thought and morality. But is either picture true, the picture which makes Nature neutral to human right or wrong, or the picture which makes her hostile to right?

It will be enough for our purpose if we can show that the picture of her neutrality is radically distorted, and to this we shall at present confine our argument. Current idealism intimidated, I think, by the closed-system idea of Nature, is curiously vague here. It seems simply to take over the current scientific idea and include it without question in its synthesis. We may turn again for information to Professor Whitehead's review of nineteenth-century thought.

"This idealistic school . . . has swallowed the scientific scheme in its entirety as being the only rendering of the facts of Nature, and has thus explained it as being an idea in the ultimate mentality. In the case of absolute idealism, the world of nature is just one of the ideas, somehow differentiating the unity of the Absolute: in the case of pluralistic Idealism involving monadic mentalities, this world is the greatest common measure of the various ideas which differentiate the various mental unities of the various monads. But, however you take it, these idealistic schools have conspicuously failed to connect, in any organic fashion, the fact of Nature with their idealistic philosophies." [3]

In most, at least, of the versions of it familiar to me, modern idealism would come a long way short of accepting Dr Denney's sweeping statement, "The Universe is a system of things in which there is a ceaseless and unrelenting reaction against evil," as it would certainly regard the whole Biblical idea of sin leading to "death," and righteousness to "life," as an obsolete idea.

The general idea of Nature held by current idealism seems rather to be that of a resisting medium in conflict with which the human reason—speculative and practical—is kindled into a glow of intellectual and moral insight, hard experience awaking its *a priori* powers, even as the resistance of the marble awakens the slumbering genius of the sculptor. In this way the idea of Nature

[3] *Science and the Modern World*, p. 93.

as absolutely neutral is preserved, and all the stress of evolution thrown on man's reason. But the marble itself does not differentiate between the sculptor's true and false intuitions of beauty. It is passive, inert, neutral. It does not strike back at him when he goes wrong, nor reward him of itself when he goes right! But it compels him to struggle with it as Jacob struggled with the angel, and the struggle somehow develops, and awakens the man's personality and conscience, his latent powers of discovering good and evil.

This is true and profound up to a certain point. But I do not think it implies, as the Bible does, that sin always brings suffering of one kind or other, either to the sinner himself or others, or that the world is such that it reacts against men and nations who identify themselves with evil, and favours men and nations who identify themselves with good.

Now there is certainly much in man's moral nature that is utterly incapable of being derived from experience of the happy consequences of virtuous living and the tragedies that result from moral failure. The story of man's moral as of his intellectual progress is not so much the story of the making as of the awakening of personalities to the eternal environment that lies behind the natural.

But we buy our conservation of the idea that Nature is a complete and self-enclosed physical system much too dear, at the expense of the sacrifice of too many of the plain facts of the history of man's moral development, if that purchase compels us to hold to the view that Nature is morally neutral towards human right and wrong, and concerned simply with maintaining her own uniform and orderly physical working.

At first sight, it is true, the facts appear to bear out this view so irresistibly that there seems no need to suppose that we need attribute it to any such far-fetched cause as the laboratory concept of the closed system of Nature. Does not simple observation of everyday life compel the view of the inhuman neutrality of Nature to man's good and evil deeds, and contradict the crude old idea that sin leads to death ?—

> Yet even when man forsakes
> All sin,—is just, is pure,
> Abandons all which makes
> His welfare insecure,—
> Other existences there are that clash with ours.
>
> Streams will not curb their pride
> The just man not to entomb,
> Nor lightnings go aside
> To give his virtues room :
> Nor is that wind less rough
> That blows a good man's barge.
>
> Nature with equal mind
> Sees all her sons at play ;
> Sees man control the wind,
> The wind sweep man away ;
> Allows the proudly riding and the foundering bark.[4]

Yet, somehow, the same writer constantly asserted, as has been said above, there is " a Power not ourselves that makes for righteousness." We may fairly ask, " What does He *do* ? "

[4] M. Arnold's *Empedocles on Etna*

All that the poet has said may be true and yet Nature may be anything but neutral in man's struggle between good and evil, truth and falsehood. It is perfectly true that our individual goodness or badness makes only occasionally any difference to our personal expectation of life. No insurance company makes any such inquiry into the virtues of its clients as it does into their physical constitution. It sounds their lungs and their hearts, and inquires if they are of a sedentary occupation or expect to be travelling in tropical regions. There are, of course, exceptions to this rule. It does inquire if they are temperate, and it looks carefully for any trace of venereal poisoning. But it makes no inquiry as to truth, humility, courage, or justice.

Such considerations are supposed to close the whole question as to the moral neutrality of Nature to man's good or evil, and to make obsolete the whole Biblical idea of the relation between sin and death, righteousness and life. But we must, surely, go deeper. If we do so we shall discover a great assumption which conceals a fatal fallacy. All our popular current ways of looking at the matter take for granted the existence of a stable and ordered civil society, and the average lease of life that we have under such a condition. We never think of anything else, or provide for any other condition. The schedules of insurance companies, in Western lands at least, do not lay their account with possible cataclysms of the heaven or earth, earthquakes, typhoons, and sweeping pestilences. These are supposed to be beyond normal probability. Yet if such shattering calamities happened which broke up the stable order of society, and resolved it into "a huddle of unrelated units," individuals striving desperately for dear life by the strength of their hands and the cunning of their brains, what would the expectation of life be then? We make a similar assumption about great moral apostasies, and this assumption conceals the basal realities, however convenient it may be in practice.

But instead of such paralysing calamities falling on society from without, suppose that by a sudden unseen apostasy the virtues were blotted out from men's hearts and nothing left but the animal instincts of self-assertion, hunger, and lust, society would be suddenly dissolved from within. The normal expectation of life would vanish, and the reign of death be swift and appalling. The world would reek with mortality as certainly as it does when there is an earthquake. The triumph of sin would mean the triumph of death. In such a case would it be any longer possible to maintain the ethical neutrality of Nature? At every turn she would be bringing home to our horrified senses the close and vital relation between the world within, the world of moral evil and good, and the world without, the world of suffering and death. That relation is under normal circumstances concealed from us because we take for granted a certain average of virtue and self-command in civilised society. We have had an appalling reminder of how thin is the conventional crust of "normal expectations" in the Great War. I do not know how the life insurance companies met it! But I am certain that it shattered all their ordinary tables. It was the most colossal illustration in civilised history of sin working death.

Why then should we talk of the moral neutrality of Nature, or of Nature's being a closed system in which every physical event can be completely explained in terms of its purely physical antecedents, irrespective of our exertions or volitions? Could the physical death resulting from such a hypothetical moral apostasy as I have imagined be explained in terms of purely physical antecedents? Such very obvious considerations inevitably lead us to feel that both the current popular science and the ordinary version of idealism have somehow got out of touch with the realities of human experience and history. Nature must be less neutral in man's education than they imagine.

That type of idealism here, which, to use Dr Denney's phrase, regards Nature as simply the stage on which the moral life was transacted, has therefore at this point laid itself fatally open to the criticism of the naturalistic evolutionary school. These writers, following in the wake of Darwin, have denied the necessity of presupposing any *a priori* element in morality. Morality is fundamentally a racial character which men have developed in the struggle for existence. It is the product of natural selection as much as the beak and claw of the bird of prey. The peoples who have developed an adequate social structure and a moral character adequate to the sustaining of that social structure survive, because they are the strongest and fittest to survive.

The others do not, because having no adequate morality, they cannot maintain a vigorous social life. Moral duties are thus resolved into racial expediences. They have been driven home to man's mind by the tremendous discipline of events, the remorseless penalties which Nature has enforced on the peoples who refused to obey them, and the rewards which she has bestowed on those who practise them. These penalties falling upon anarchic, apathetic, and decadent peoples, and through them striking at the individuals of which they are composed, are of many kinds—privation, pestilence, famine, and enslavement. But all penalties are privations of life, and behind them is the supreme penalty of death. Such in substance is the naturalistic evolutionary theory of morality.

Its real value lies not in the naturalistic philosophy with which it has been associated, which is already passing into the twilight, but in the fresh contact with the facts, and in particular the new and closer study of the influence of the environment, the development of Anthropology, Sociology, and Comparative Ethics, which the rise of the evolutionary theory has brought about. I do not think that it is possible reasonably to deny that Natural Selection has played a great part in the development of human society and morality.

Least of all do I see why religious thought should find any difficulty in granting and welcoming this view, for it represents in a most drastic and unexpected way a return to the Biblical idea that sin works death, and that God educates the human race by the consequences of its own actions. The testimony to the truth of this ancient principle is all the more impressive as nothing was further from the thoughts of those who first advanced and who have laboured at the demonstration of the evolutionary theory. They got their theory from a fresh and a more thorough study of the facts of Nature, primitive and savage man, and history.

When we come to ask the further question of whether the theory of Natural Selection taken alone can account for all the facts of the moral life, I think we must say that it fails conspicuously to do so. It has been present as a mighty and persistent factor in the development, but, when all is said, an external factor only. It has not created the moral consciousness of man. It has awakened, developed, and conserved it. On all this part of the debate the idealistic answer seems to me sufficient and conclusive. We cannot get out of Natural Selection and the evolutionary process above either the full moral imperative or the intrinsic values which are revealed in conscience. The evolutionary account of morality can explain only the protective husk under which the moral reason of man, which tells him the difference between right and wrong, grows up to maturity.

Dr Rashdall has put the distinction with humour as well as truth.

"Evolution," he says, "does not produce our geometrical ideas; they are only producible in a mind already potentially endowed with a capacity for apprehending them. And so with moral ideas. It would be as absurd to talk about 'the struggle for existence' and 'natural selection' as constituting by themselves the 'origin' of our moral ideas, as it would be to treat the cane of the schoolmaster as being the 'origin' of our geometrical ideas, though there may be persons in whom these ideas would never have been developed without that agency. Moralities could have developed only in beings endowed with a capacity for Moral Reason; and the truths of which our Moral Reason assures us are not less true because we recognise that certain biological facts and processes have been the condition of their discovery by this or that individual in this or that generation. Moral ideas are no more 'produced' or generated by physical events than any other of the categories of human thought. When this is recognised, there should be no hesitation in admitting that all the biological and psychological and social facts insisted on by the evolutionary moralists have really been conditions of moral development. They really do help to explain why such a virtue was developed at such a time and place, and another virtue in different circumstances, why this aspect of morality was emphasised in one kind of community and another in another, and so forth." [5]

With this admission I entirely agree. There is no reason whatever why the most convinced Idealist should not only "admit," but should most cordially welcome the great service which the evolutionary moralists have done by bringing us into fresh contact with the facts of human life and history by calling attention to the great part which natural selection has played in awakening the

[5] *Theory of Good and Evil*, vol. ii. pp. 99-100.

human spirit to the perception of the moral order of the Universe, as well as in developing the human mind in the knowledge of eternal truth.

But if this be so, the whole popular theory of the moral neutrality of nature must go by the board, and disappear submerged by the overwhelming advance of knowledge. To say that Natural Selection, broadly regarded, selects the more highly advanced types of society, and, broadly regarded, destroys the decadent and morally torpid peoples, to establish this as a general law, in spite of apparent exceptions, is to take a long step towards recognising not only that "Nature" is anything but "morally neutral," but that the world is under moral government, and that God educates men in truth and goodness not only through other men, but by the consequences of their own actions, in other words, by the rewards and retaliations of the natural environment.

Have the greatest intuitive and imaginative writers ever held anything else? Have they ever succumbed to the dreary fallacy that nature was wholly neutral in the great drama of the human spirit?

Æschylus, Dante, Shakespeare—have they not all made us feel that the nature of things is remorselessly on the side of justice, mercy, and truth? That sin within works death and woe without, that there is a close inner relation between them, is part of the very substance of their thought, and has inspired the deepest notes of their music. All this is really unthinkable on the supposition of an absolutely neutral nature. Nature is far too closely inwoven with the psychical life of man to admit of anything of the kind. The system of Nature and human life is to the synthetic genius of the poets one and not two dissevered though parallel parts, and they, like all the great Biblical writers, believe that the wages of sin is death. I do not say that the great humanists teach this in any narrow way in their tragedies. They recognise the sufferings of the innocent, and the apparent inequalities of justice in the mysterious whole of the world. But the undertone is more or less, I think, the same in all the greatest.

I do not claim, and for our immediate purpose it is not necessary to claim, that the evolutionary idealistic interpretation of man's ethical training is identical with the Biblical interpretation. It would be, indeed, surprising if it were. The evolutionists and the Biblical writers approach the facts of life from quite distinct points of view, and use different methods. The religious interpretation of life, of which we have the classical form in the Old and New Testaments, comes down, as it were, upon the world from the idea of God. It has reached the faith in His ethical nature and in His sovereign control of all things. It therefore seeks to explain the facts of life in terms of this growing faith. In the Old Testament and in the New we have a great labour of thought expended on this study of human life *sub specie æternitatis*. We see this interpretation growing out of its first crude form by honest facing of all the facts, and passing out at last into its fully developed form in the New Testament. It is what William James called "the personal and romantic view of life," which recognises personality, individuality, the living relation of God with living human beings in mercy and in judgment and in Fatherly care. The modern scientific view begins with human beings, and proceeds like every science by way of the inductive methods. It makes abstraction from all particulars, and, dwelling on all common characteristics, it reaches out after general laws.

It is surely perfectly clear that the last thing we ought to expect is complete coincidence between the two accounts. To do so would be as absurd as to expect identity of detail in pictures of a mountain range taken from two totally different points of view. Yet, for all that, both may be absolutely true pictures. All that we have a right to look for is such general agreement as will enable us to see that the object pictured is the same.

Now I do not see how we can possibly maintain that the view of the "cosmic process" given us by Huxley, in which "Nature" is represented as fighting against man's higher life, can be brought into any harmony with the religious interpretation. It is radically inconsistent with the Divine Providence. Further, I do not see how the view which regards Nature as neutral to man's higher life can be brought into harmony with the Biblical view in its full Christian form. It is also radically inconsistent with the Christian ideas of providence and prayer. The inevitable result of trying to combine views so divergent must be to mutilate either the religious or the scientific interpretations or both.

But on the view which I have endeavoured to set forth in this chapter, there seems to me to be no such contradiction, but rather a deep and surprising agreement.

For on both views alike, Nature is anything but neutral, it takes sides definitely with those peoples who stake their lives on essential morality. Both views, also, alike recognise that the penalties of wrongdoing and false thinking and intellectual sloth are not necessarily inflicted on the wrong-doer or false thinker himself, but often, though not always, on the community to which he belongs. It matters not that the scientific view ascribes this to the organic character of society, or to "solidarity," and the religious view speaks of vicarious suffering, for in principle the two ideas are the same.

I believe, therefore, that that appalling contradiction which Mill, Huxley, and Russell found to exist between the alien cosmic order which they discerned with their senses and understanding, and the world of moral values of which they were inwardly aware, has just as little existence as that supposed neutrality and self-sufficiency of Nature which more idealistic thought teaches; and that, on the contrary, we have, with all remaining difficulties, good reason to believe, as Christian thought has always believed, that Nature is dependent upon God, is purposive throughout towards His spiritual ends, and that it is plastic in His hands for the guidance and discipline of free human spirits. I admit that what we have is faith rather than demonstration, that there are unsolved problems in the disharmonies of Nature and the tragedies of human life, and that our knowledge of the stupendous whole is exceedingly limited. Yet we know enough to be morally certain that we hold the clue to the labyrinth in the ideal ends of Truth, Beauty, and Goodness, in the knowledge and pursuit of which and of Him in whom they are One "standeth our eternal life, whose service is perfect freedom," and that great Nature, far from being hostile or neutral to these ideal ends, is in the long run decisively on their side.

Let us now draw together the threads of our argument, and consider the bearing of its results on the question of our Lord's miracles.

If that argument has been sound, the positive evils which man endures from the great system of Nature are contingent either upon his departure from true and worthy ways of thinking and living, or his failure to attain them. They are all in their Divine intention revelatory of the true order, and therefore educative. And inasmuch as God wills this perfection for all His children, they are contingent upon a condition of man's heart and mind which is not in conformity with God's purpose for him. They are not parts of the Divine and eternal order at all. They are, on any thoroughgoing Theistic view of the world, signs that man has not as yet attained that depth and width of knowledge, and sufficient purity and loyalty of heart as son of God and brother of men in the great human family or Kingdom of God, which he is meant to attain. All this seems to me to follow quite naturally and inevitably from the faith that "the world is not a vale of tears, but a place of soul-making." That again follows inevitably from the Fatherhood of God as revealed by Jesus Christ. But if this fundamental view of the spiritual ground, nature, and purpose of the world be true, and if the natural evils of life are signs that man has not yet attained full spiritual maturity, then it would seem to follow, that if Jesus of Nazareth were the true Son of God, the ideal human being whom they depict Him to have been, it was fitting that He should do just the kind of works that they declare Him to have done, and show Himself uniquely master of those natural evils.

And on the other hand, if He did what He is reported to have done, He has definitely verified that general view of the world as created by God, as directed by His will towards the realisation of His Kingdom, and as meantime plastic in His Hands for the everyday protection and discipline of His children, in which Jesus Himself demonstrably lived and moved and had His being.

CHAPTER VI

MODERN INSTANCES AND SPECULATIONS

We have nearly worked our way through to the point where we may claim to have established a case for using the miracles of Jesus Christ to interrogate the universe; for asking what light they have to throw upon the courses of nature and history, the character and purpose of God, the place and power of prayer and the ultimate destiny of man.

But it may be said that the argument has been vitiated by one great omission. It implies that the power of Christ over Nature and, in particular, over the destroying and mortal powers of Nature inhere in His perfect humanity through which the Holy Spirit, the Lord and Giver of Life, can work deeds of creative life and blessing in the lives of men. But if it be so, we should surely expect to find in His followers some trace at least of that supernatural power, however faintly and imperfectly it may manifest itself. Now it is said, it is matter of plain fact that these lives manifest nothing of the kind. They do show, in general, some signs of inward regenerating power, and, sometimes, changes of character so radical that the best language for describing them is that of new birth. But there is nothing at all of the same kind in the outward life, nothing physical corresponding to the spiritual deliverances of which religious biography is full. Do we, indeed, expect to return to the age of miracles? This is, indeed, the practical crux of the whole argument.

First of all in reply to the last question, I would say that it depends entirely on what is meant by "miracles." As the word is usually employed, it would mean, Do we expect that the time is at hand when men will do the things that Jesus did? I would say, "Assuredly, no." The whole argument implies that these extraordinary achievements of prayer were due to His extraordinary spiritual personality which was so entirely at one with the will of the Father that the Father was able to do extraordinary deeds of blessing, through Him. The difference between His achievements and the greatest of other men's achievements is a measure of the spiritual difference between Him and them. It is like the difference between Shakespeare and some modern playwright.

But if by "miracle" we mean something inexplicable in terms of physical Nature, I would say, "Assuredly, yes." In this sense every free human action, as Lord Kelvin once said, is a miracle, for it cannot be accounted for in terms of its merely physical antecedents. As we have seen, the power of the sciences to explain all individuality and the physical actions that result from individuality is far less than men used to believe. In this sense, too, every answered prayer is a miracle. I believe that such miracles are happening every day of our lives, and that no earnest life that lives by prayer is so poor as to be without them. I do not see any reason whatever to discredit the many instances that can be given to prove that God hears and answers prayer for outward as well as inward blessings and enhancements of life, recovery from sickness, delivery from danger and famine. I do not believe that our Lord put the prayer for daily bread in His prayer without meaning something by it.

In this sense, then, I certainly believe that we are one and all meant to work miracles, and that they are occurring all around us only they are not recognised as such.

But, further, it has to be said that to a great extent modern men and women have ceased to ask for and expect them, largely owing to sophistications and perplexities in the region of thought. In current experience they are most commonly to be found on the mission field remote from the influence of the Time Spirit, in the lives of devout men and women who live apart from the great intellectual currents, or in communities like the Friends who are nurtured in a tradition of "signs and wonders" in the life of the Spirit.

I do not believe that this limitation of faith in prayer is likely to be anything but a passing phase in the life of true Christendom. It is due in part to that intellectual sophistication of which I have spoken, and in part to that weakening of the idea of God which is the radical spiritual malady of our time and is the real cause of that peculiar flatness and deadness of the life of the Church, of which so many with greater or less justice complain.

It is surely too much that an age like ours should take its own life and achievement as the normal standard, and rule out of the New Testament as myth, legend and overbelief, all for which it can find no strict analogy in the life of to-day. The underlying assumption is that our own spiritual climate is that which is normal for the human race, an odd self-complacency for an age the natural working out of whose ideals and methods has produced so enormous a conflagration as the world war. Nearly all the deepest judges of our age tell us that it has been an age in which the higher forces of the Spirit are running low.

Can we pass beyond that general answer that we who believe in God know that prayer is answered?

Is there anything in the progress of human knowledge that brings the signs of Jesus more within the range of what is believable by modern men? Or are we in that respect just in the same position as were the men and women of fifty years ago? I have already pointed out that there has been a very great though only half-realised or acknowledged change here in the general position of the modernist school which indicates quite plainly that new facts of that kind have come to light. In the days of Strauss and Renan nearly all the miracles of Jesus were regarded as either mythical or legendary. To-day one great exception is almost invariably made. The healing miracles are in substance admitted to be probably true history. That is a very remarkable fact. There cannot be the least doubt as to the cause of this change. It is due to nothing less than the growing conviction that there is clear and convincing evidence that there is undeniable reality in some at least of the innumerable stories of cures of bodily disease by spiritual means which have been recorded from a great variety of sources within the last eighty years.

At first these stories came purely from religious sources. The Roman Church was early[1] in the field with the "miracles" of Lourdes, but as the nineteenth century went on Protestantism began to develop several distinct schools of spiritual healing, that of Pastor Blumhardt at Badboll, which exerted a marked influence on German opinion, certain more obscure movements in England, and finally the immense outgrowth of Christian Science in the United States.

But the deepest and widest impression on the educated mind was made when science took the matter up and the growing interest in and understanding of the phenomena of hypnotism led to the rise of psycho-therapeutics. The steady accumulation of facts in this domain at last forced the recognition that the mind was more concerned both in the production and in the healing of disease than the older medical science had been prepared to recognise, and than the old hard and fast philosophical dualism of conscious mind and unconscious body could admit. Frederick Myers's volumes on *Human Personality* first brought the idea of the subliminal region within the ken of

[1] Of course the Roman Church has never abandoned the claim that miracles were wrought by the saints and at certain holy places. But Lourdes is her most conspicuous modern instance.

the English-speaking public, and gave the ordinary man a new pigeon-hole in which he could now receive and store the strange and hitherto "occult" facts which were too well attested for him to deny. Next came the schools of Freud and Jung, and then came the war and its tragic multitudes of nerve-shattered men with maladies with which the older types of medical science, however magnificently successful they were in their own regions, proved utterly unable to cope, while the newer methods of psycho-therapeutics often proved completely successful.

I once, after the close of the war, asked one of the most distinguished authorities on these methods what difference it had made to him and his fellow practitioners. "Just this," he said, "that at the beginning of the war we found it impossible to get a chance in the field, and that now we cannot get demobilised."

To-day it is generally, I think, conceded by most open-minded people that many diseases even of the body can be successfully attacked from within through the mind, as well as from without through the body.

How far that attack may be successfully made there is no general argeement, even among experts in psycho-therapeutic treatment. One of these told the writer that there were certain forms of physical disease that he had no hope that with his methods he could ever cure, while another,[2] equally distinguished, was positive that ideally

[2] Both of these men were fully qualified medical practitioners, and distinguished men of science.

every form of disease could be successfully treated by such methods, "though," he added, "it will take a good while to do it. I do not expect that in twenty-five years from now we shall be treating cancer by suggestion, but by a new serum." Orthodox medical science, while admitting that there is no tissue of the human body that may not be influenced by spirit, draws the line between functional and organic disease. Bolder spirits in the other camp argue that this distinction in kind is arbitrary and depends simply and solely on the fact that our microscopes are as yet not of sufficient power to reveal organic deterioration in all functionally disordered tissues, and so to make the distinction simply one of degree.

All genuinely religious faith in spiritual healing, of course, while it admits the distinction, denies its relevance. "With God all things are possible." Meantime facts accumulate. Each one interested must examine the evidence for himself as he may meet with it in his own experience or study it in the voluminous but somewhat loosely attested reports in the periodical publications of Christian Science, or the more carefully drawn up volumes and bulletins which originate at Lourdes. I confess that unless one possesses a comfortable *a priori* theory which enables one satisfactorily to decide as to what is or is not true beforehand, it is extremely difficult to escape from the conclusion that diseases usually called organic sometimes yield to these methods as certainly as many that are called functional. I would recommend to any one who doubts this a careful study of one or more of the Lourdes volumes to which I have referred above, which always give the previous medical diagnosis and which certify the results. It is easy to check these by reading the hostile literature, which is also voluminous. As a matter of fact, so far as mere scientific evidence goes some of these " miracles " are better attested than some in the Gospels themselves.

Few people who have not examined the evidence which is now available on the whole matter have any idea of the change in the whole outlook on the possibilities of the powers of the mind over the body which the last twenty-five years have effected.

I shall content myself however with two quotations on the matter from Professor Macdougall's well-known volume on *Body and Mind*.

" It has been shown that under certain conditions (especially in the hypnotic and post-hypnotic states) the mind may exert an influence over the organic processes of the body far greater than any that had been generally recognised by physiologists. Especially noteworthy are the production of blisters, erythemata and ecchymoses of the skin (the so-called stigmata [3]) in positions and of definite shapes determined by verbal suggestions, and the rapid healing of wounds or burns with almost complete suppression of inflammation; and with these may be put the complete suppression or prevention of pain, even pain of such severity as normally accompanies a major surgical operation." [4]

Professor Macdougall brings his massive survey of the entire field of the relations between mind and body to a conclusion in a chapter from which the

[3] *Sc.* of St Francis and others. [4] P. 351.

following carefully guarded sentence is taken. It seems to me to represent the real state of the question on the particular point under immediate discussion. "Successful therapeutic suggestions and others that effect definite tissue changes are especially significant in the present connexion; for in all such cases we have definite evidence of control of bodily processes which, though unconsciously effected, must be regarded as psychical. Of the limits of this power of mental control over the organic processes of the body we are altogether ignorant, and new evidence, much of it ill reported, and therefore valueless, but much of it above suspicion, repeatedly warns us against setting up any arbitrary limit to what may be effected in this way."[5]

It is impossible to study all this immensely varied mass of evidence coming from all the different schools of spiritual and mental healing and psychotherapeutics without being impressed by its superficial diversity and its fundamental agreement as to method. There is the sharpest antagonism between the schools of practitioners. To the devout Roman Catholic the whole claim of Protestant faith-healers and Christian Scientists is anathema, and there is chronic warfare also between him and the physicians of the Salpetrière and the school of Nancy. To the true Christian Scientist there is only one scientific method of healing, and that is his own; hypnotism in particular is of the pit. To the psycho-therapeutist, Christian Scientists and faith-healers are blundering fanatics or charlatans. Yet there is one

[5] Pp. 374-5.

fundamental thing that they all alike call for and that one thing is Faith. They one and all ask for a belief in the healer or the suggestion or the ultimate nature of things so full that it shall generate in the imagination the confident expectation that the thing sought for will be given, or, better still, that it has already been given, and that all that is needed is to realise it. In other words, they ask for a kind of faith and hope. That this is so any one can verify for himself by studying the copious literature of all these movements and schools. This agreement seems to me of extraordinary significance, and taken in connection with what was said at the beginning of this chapter about those answers to prayers "of which many can testify," it disposes completely of the objection that there is nothing in human nature and experience as we know them to-day which would warrant us in believing that if we were liker Christ we might in some measure share His powers over the mortal forces of Nature. Something has happened in the world of the last fifty years, the discovery of latent potentialities in human nature, which throws new light on this ancient controversy, something which was not fully before the mind of either the earlier Traditionalist or Modernist when they framed their views of the miracles of Jesus.

Many good people to-day think that it lowers the greatness of the miracles of Jesus to seek to bring them into any kind of comparison with Lourdes and Christian Science and Spiritual Healing and Psychotherapeutics. They are thus at the opposite pole from those referred to above, whose main difficulty with the miracles of Jesus is that there is nothing in human experience that is in the least analogous with them, nothing that helps us to believe that even a Personality unique in greatness and goodness can have any greater influence for good on the world of Nature than the most commonplace personality and the meanest character. I confess that I do not share the difficulty of the former class. There is a profound difference between the deeds of Jesus taken as a whole and the miracles of Lourdes and Nancy, but so far as physical results go it is a difference of degree rather than of kind.

I would plead for a more sympathetic outlook on all these strange phenomena of spiritual and mental healing. If they can be finally established as true facts, the result would be greatly to enrich human life and widen and deepen our whole view of the world. They show that even in this world spiritual and mental forces can control for good the lower forces, and that a bold and generous faith in the ultimate nature of things works for physical, as we know that it does for mental and spiritual, soundness and health. If these facts can be established and set beyond all doubt, I cannot but think it would be a good day for the human race. The world would be proved to be a richer and finer place for humanity to dwell in, more sympathetic and responsive to human need. That these phenomena have been often exploited by fanatics and charlatans is nothing to the point. There is no field of human science that in its earlier stages has not been so exploited. Did not astronomy grow out of astrology, and chemistry from the quest for the philosopher's stone? The facts and their attestation or disproof are what we have to fix our thoughts upon, and if, as seems now indisputable, disease can be dispelled or even alleviated from the spiritual side by means of ordinary human beings to-day, that has a very momentous and definite bearing upon the historical character of the healing miracles of the Gospels, which it is mere obscurantism to ignore.

It may be granted by others that while all this may be true of what is known as spiritual healing, it is not true of the cures wrought by suggestion under hypnosis or of psycho-therapeutics; that these have nothing whatever in common with the miracles of healing recorded in the Gospels, and that therefore they cannot be brought into the question at all. It is quite true that these have often nothing distinctively religious about them, and often seem almost as mechanical as cures wrought by the action of a drug. Waiving, for the moment, the point to which I have already referred, that the patient must have some measure of faith in the healer and his method and in the suggestion given him, I would point out that every one of the miracles of the Gospels must have had a psychological side. Assuming the truth of the New Testament view that all our Lord's deeds of healing were wrought by the Spirit of God, there must have been some point at which that Heavenly Life made contact with and influenced the human organism, and set in operation the psychophysical processes of renewal. Psycho-therapeutics has explored this region and shown that it is still open to the control of the mind.[6]

As has been said, the impression made upon modern thought by the phenomena of which I have spoken has been sufficiently great to make most if not all modern writers on the life of Jesus admit in general terms the historical credibility of His healing miracles. This change is of itself sufficient to dispose of the difficulty stated at the beginning of this chapter. But here the line is usually drawn. The nature miracles, as they are called, the narratives of the stilling of the storm and the feeding of the multitudes, are still regarded as incredible and, therefore, legendary. The reason is obvious. Modern experience has given us something analogous to the healing miracles. But to these there is believed to be no parallel. They are "signs" wrought, not upon responsive human bodies, but directly on the great frame of Nature herself, and one of them at least seems to be a miracle not of influence and direction of natural forces, but of actual creation. The distinction is held to be so great as to make such miracles unbelievable by modern men and women. Many even of those who fully accept the uniqueness of Christ and the reality of His healing miracles are willing to give up these nature miracles as inconsistent with the scientific outlook and also as

[6] I leave meantime undiscussed the question of what it is that in the last resort heals in psycho-therapeutic treatment, whether, as is commonly said, it is the suggestion that heals, or whether it simply puts the mind and the psycho-physical mechanisms in such a relation to the cosmos that healing influences can enter.

contributing little or nothing to the Christian interpretation of life. But is it indeed so? With reference to the former point there does not appear to me to be any difference in principle between these nature miracles and the healing miracles. Neither group can really be brought within the "closed system" of physical Nature. While, like the others, the nature miracles elude physical science, they may well belong to history, for once more we have to remember the unique personality of Jesus.

It is quite true that a sign wrought upon the vast frame of Nature, as it were directly, seems much greater, more out of the common, than one wrought upon the human body. The human body seems something intermediate between nature and spirit. It seems to be a piece of nature half spiritualised already, and therefore more readily open to spiritual influences. But we must think clearly and consecutively. The consistent scientific naturalism with which we have mainly to do cannot admit that the body is open to spiritual influences. Body and spirit are parallel processes, lines that never meet, and therefore the body is just as sealed to spiritual influences as are the winds and the waters. The whole of physical Nature is one closed system under the complete sway of material causation throughout, or no part of it is. But if we depart, as we have seen reason to depart, from this view, if we have made up our minds that it is an incomplete view of Nature, then it no longer stands in the way of even the "nature miracles" of Jesus.

Nothing can be more futile when great issues are before us which demand coherent thought, than to grant the possibility of small miracles and to hold to the impossibility of great. Consistent religious thought finds it difficult to treat such reasoning seriously. It is like pleading in defence of a murder that the person murdered was only a child. The reply of the law is that it was murder all the same.

But when we have thus cleared the ground of the strictly scientific and relevant difficulty, and when the argument is with those who no longer stand by the "closed system" conception of nature, as anything but a convenient method and calculus of thought, with those who have a freer and more spiritual view of the universe, Theistic in its bases, with men who admit that the body is the meeting-ground of Nature and Spirit and that from the spiritual side influences directing, moulding and renewing do pass over into the physical, we may readily admit that there is some difference between the healing and the nature miracles. There is a greater difficulty for the imagination in believing that Christ said to the storm and the waves, "Peace be still!" and that they obeyed Him, than that He said, "Rise, take up thy bed and walk!" and that the paralytic "arose and followed Him." We think of the miracles of healing as wrought directly by Jesus on men's bodies through their minds, but we see no such mental bridge between Christ and the storm. The difficulty suggests a deepening of all our thought about healing and nature miracles alike. Are they not all alike wrought through the

Divine mind by prayer? For anyone who believes in the living God in whom nature has its origin and who controls its course is there really any fundamental difficulty that is not present in the other case? I do not think so. In the one case as in the other it is really God who heals the body and controls the storm, and it is in His name that Jesus utters His commands.

But it may be said, are the nature miracles of any real spiritual importance? On the view which I have been endeavouring to set forth in this volume, as that of the Gospels themselves, they certainly are. When all is said, physical disease is only one of the multitude of natural ills to which man is at present subject—plague, hunger, and the wild forces of Nature, symbolised in the sea and the storm. The nature miracles are indications that subjection to none of these things is part of God's unconditional will for man. They have no place in the Kingdom of God. Man's present subjection to them and the havoc and sorrow that they cause in human life is due to his imperfection, ignorance, and sin. They are therefore part of his discipline in character and in knowledge, in faith and in prayer. But we have no reason to believe that permanent subjection to them is part of the unchangeable, unconditional will of God for men. It is not impious for men to fight against famine, or foolish for men to pray for deliverance from the storm. It is indeed their duty to do both, just as it is their duty to strive and pray against the inroads of disease.

Has real piety of the Biblical type ever thought

anything else, or shrunk from the appeal to God to control even the winds and the waters and deliver those "in peril on the sea"? These prayers are certainly for something more than that those in such peril may be kept calm and strong and morally intact amid their dangers. They should include that, but they are for real objective deliverance, and that, as we have seen, necessarily implies something over and above the "closed system" of nature, something in principle, therefore, "miraculous" in the broader meaning of the term, in other words a nature miracle.

In truth the real difficulty which many feel about the nature miracles of Jesus has precisely the same root as that difficulty which many feel about petitionary prayer for anything save inward spiritual help and guidance. We have here the old obsession about the "closed system" of physical nature showing itself once more. That "closed system" is assumed to be the whole of Nature, and is then identified with the immovable decree of God. From the point of view of the argument of this book the nature miracles of Jesus are needed to complete the idea embodied in the healing miracles. They are meant to embody the ideal will of God and the ideal destiny of man in the Kingdom of Heaven. Our Lord's resurrection is the crowning manifestation of that victory over all the mortal and tragic powers of the world. It unites the two groups of His signs of which I have spoken. On the one hand it may be classed with the healing group, for all disease is a kind of dying. On the other, a human body from which life has departed seems simply part of the inorganic world,

> Rolled round in earth's diurnal course
> With rocks and stones and trees.

It is as much part of the dead material world as the winds and waters of the Galilean lake. It is difficult to see, if we reject the nature miracles on principle, how we can continue to maintain a reasonable faith in the complete reality of the resurrection. Yet a Christianity without a true resurrection is bereft, as I have tried to show, of something that lies near the very springs of its genius. Modernist attempts to show that the first Christians did not believe in anything but a spiritual resurrection of Jesus, an escape to God from the trammels of the body, come dangerously near to special pleading. It can be quite conclusively shown, for instance, that the idea of the body as the prison of the soul is not Hebrew at all but Greek. It can be shown also, quite conclusively, that the whole structure of Hebrew and Jewish thought compelled men to hold that Christ's premature death upon the Cross demanded a full and complete resurrection, and an empty tomb, if His disciples were to recover their faith in Him as the victorious Messiah and the "prince of life" they believed Him to be. Such considerations compel us to take St Paul's words [7] in their natural way and at their full value. "I delivered unto you first of all that which also I received: that Christ died for our sins according

[7] 1 Cor. xv. 3 and 4.

to the Scriptures; and that he was buried, and that he hath been raised on the third day according to the Scriptures."

It has been argued that St Paul here is thinking only of a spiritual resurrection of Jesus and that it is significant that he makes no mention of the empty tomb. I have already in another connection [8] dealt with this argument, but something falls to be added. Dr Denney's reply to this ingenuity is, I think, final. "The mention of the burial is important in this connection as defining what is meant by the rising—we see from it that it would have conveyed no meaning to Paul or any member of the original Christian circle to say that it was the spirit of Christ which rose to new life, or that He rose again in the faith of His devoted followers, who could not bear the thought that for Him death should end all. The rising is relative to the grave and the burial, and if we cannot speak of a bodily resurrection we should not speak of a resurrection at all." [9]

It is, as has already been pointed out, difficult to see how anyone who has really studied St Paul's whole thought on the relation between sin and death, on the body and the spirit, and finally on the ultimate transformation of the body, can persuade himself that St Paul could possibly have believed in any theory of the Lord's resurrection which could dispense with the empty tomb. We are not at the moment concerned with the truth or error of these Pauline ideas, but simply with the kind of resurrection in which he believed. It is

[8] Pp. 44-45. [9] *Jesus and the Gospels*, p. 113.

quite clear from the whole context of his thought, as well as from his own words, that at the centre of his faith lay the full Easter message, and that in this he was at one with the whole New Testament community. This full resurrection faith is the very root of the New Testament optimism. There is no more characteristic expression of it than the opening of the first Epistle of Peter, "Blessed be the God and Father of our Lord Jesus Christ, who hath begotten us again unto a living hope by the resurrection of Jesus Christ from the dead."

There was something more here than even that which was the central and supreme thing in the New Testament consciousness—the sense that the power of sin was broken. There was the sense that the power of sorrow and tragedy was broken too, that in the resurrection the Kingdom of Heaven had been manifested to men. In a word the resurrection was the same kind of thing in a supreme and perfect way that the earlier signs of the Lord had been, the visualising of the eternal life, the first-fruits of the Spirit, the beginning of the new heaven and the new earth in which sin and sorrow would pass away and death be no more. The first Christians believed that they were living in the dawn of a new creation. The sun had risen behind them and was transfiguring earth and sky and sea with a light which would one day irradiate the whole universe. That sun was God in Christ, the risen Christ "who had abolished death and brought life and immortality to light through the Gospel."

Can we translate that idea of the resurrection

into terms of modern thought, so that we shall not miss its essence, as I cannot but think that even the well-intended mediating theories do?

It is clear that St Paul held neither these nor the simple reanimation view. He obviously believed that a transfiguring change had passed over the body of the Lord. We have here something that goes quite beyond all our experience. We admit this of all the signs of Jesus, and it is truest of all of His final victory over death. But while we freely admit this, it is permissible to approach the mystery along the lines of analogy with what we do know. If we follow the lines of organic evolution up to man, and from the most primitive men of whom we have traces up to the highest men we know, we see the bodily elements growing more and more capable of becoming instruments of Spirit, the wonderful tool of the body becoming more and more adequate for the uses of the intelligence, the imagination, and the soul. What is the difference between the monkey's paw and the artist's hand? Is there not more here than the anatomist and the physiologist can tell us, something that only comes into view when we ask as to the end? Is not the artist's hand a better expression and instrument of the spirit? Are we to suppose that the long process of the subordination of matter to spirit ends with the human body as we know it, or must there not be something more perfect still in the way of bodily organisation, a more spiritual and lasting type of body in touch with a finer and larger environment?

Such an idea sixty years ago would have been treated as simply a forlorn and "devout imagination" by the dominant science and philosophy. But to-day there come new voices from science. As regards higher forms of living organism which may transcend mortality, let us hear Bergson as he contemplates the giant stream of life pouring from the unknown past to the unknown future: "As the smallest grain of dust is bound up with our entire solar system, drawn along with it in that undivided movement of descent which is materiality itself, so all organised beings from the humblest to the highest, from the first origin of life to the time in which we are, and in all places as in all times, do but evidence a single impulsion, the inverse of the movement of matter, and in itself indivisible. All the living hold together, and all yield to the same tremendous push. The animal takes its stand upon the plant, man bestrides animality, and the whole of humanity, in space and in time, is one immense army, galloping beside and before and behind each of us in an overwhelming charge, able to beat down every resistance and clear the most formidable obstacles, perhaps even death."[10]

Let us hear another living philosophic thinker on the possibilities of the human spirit: "We need not fear that this mechanism (*i.e.* of the material world) will be found too rigid and mechanical, that in the ripeness of time it will put an absolute limit upon spiritual evolution. The time may come when Matter will no longer offer any obstacle to our wishes, and when, in sober truth, Man will

[10] *Creative Evolution*, Eng. tr., pp. 285, 286.

precipitate a mountain into the sea. Or can it be that a completer harmony of the human with the Divine Will can anticipate the course of social evolution, and give to saints and sages a power over Matter which transcends that of ordinary men, and even now enables their faith to move mountains? May not their power over Matter already rise to the level to be attained in far-distant ages, just as their intellectual and moral development towers above that of the societies in which they dwell? It is enough for a philosopher to assert that there is nothing inherently absurd in the supposition, and that a will completely synonymous with the Divine Will would needs have a complete control of the Material."[11]

And as regards the transformation of something much greater than the body, the physical universe, into what may be the environment of that transformed body, let us hear Professor Whitehead: "The universe shows us two aspects: on one side it is physically wasting, on the other it is spiritually ascending. It is thus passing with a slowness, inconceivable in our measure of time, to new creative conditions, amid which the physical world, as we at present know it, will be represented by a ripple, barely to be distinguished from non-entity."[12]

However we may speculate, the power of the resurrection faith in the first Christian age lay in this, that it was a complete victory over death and

[11] *Riddles of the Sphinx*, 2nd Edition, pp. 304-5, by F. C. S. Schiller.

[12] *Religion in the Making*, p. 160.

therefore contained in itself the promise and the potency of a like victory for all mankind. "When thou hadst overcome the sharpness of death, thou didst open the Kingdom of Heaven to all believers."

The last word then of the Gospel is not one of final submission to nature's last word, death, but of rebellion against it and of victory over it by the power of the Spirit.

CHAPTER VII

PRACTICAL DIFFICULTIES

It is clear that the general view of the miracles of the Gospels taken in this volume, as being Divine answers to the prayers of Jesus, and as being conditioned not upon His metaphysical Deity, but upon the faith, hope, and love that were in Him, carries with it certain far-reaching consequences as to the range and power of ideal prayer which must gravely affect not only our conceptions of God and the world, but which must influence deeply the practice of our devotional life. Many, I believe, will feel that the most serious difficulties lie in this region.

For one thing, it is plain that the view implies that our prayers should not be confined to purely "spiritual" matters, but should range over the whole field both of our inward and our outward lives and the lives, also, of others.

Heiler, in his remarkable book on prayer, has distinguished three types of spiritual life, the mystical, the philosophical, and the prophetic. "Mysticism must, if it remain true to itself, reject the naïve asking for external good things, and everything not directed towards (communion with) God Himself, as unworthy. The earthly is, indeed, a deceptive show without true being, something which ought not to be, a thing without value and therefore a peril for salvation and a hindrance to union with God. The affections and wishes which assert themselves must not be freely spoken out in prayer, but must be subdued, chained, and slain. The asceticism, which gradually brings to death the sensuality which feeds the emotional life of the soul, is the foundation of pure mysticism." Heiler points out, further, that philosophic and rationalist thought is also hostile to petition for earthly good and tends to reduce prayer to simple meditation. Over against these types he sets the prophetic conception of prayer which demands, not the ascetic annihilation of natural human desires and necessities, but the free opening of the whole world of human need to the Father and the simple and honest expression of these in our prayers to Him in the faith and expectation that they will be answered, not only in the spiritual, but in the whole life of man. He gives many citations from the great personalities of the Reformation and of the Evangelical faith, Luther, Calvin, Rothe, Herrmann, and others to illustrate this conception of the range and power of prayer; and sums up his review by saying, "Mysticism and the ethical philosophy found prayer for temporal good things to be irreligious and sinful. Prophetic religion, it is true, puts moral and religious values at the heart of prayer, but it has room also for the childlike and primitive prayer for life and food, for rain and sunshine."[1]

[1] *Das Gebet*, 5. Auflage, pp. 369-372. He quotes Ménégoz as saying that Kant and Hegel, Strauss and Robertson, Schleier-

The view of the Gospel teaching which has been taken in this volume emphasises this "prophetic" conception in the strongest way. The "mystical" view of prayer, indeed, can only maintain its ground either by defending the portent theory of the miracles of Jesus, or by allying itself with the modernist conception of Nature, both of which views we have seen reason to consider unsound. Neither the mystical nor the philosophical exclusion of petitionary prayer for objective good has any root in Scripture, and indeed is subtly out of harmony with the Christian idea of God. Its open or tacit acceptance by many to-day is in no way due to a mystical aloofness from the temporal needs of man. There is nothing ascetic about it. It is due, on the intellectual side, simply to our modern intimidation by the "closed system" idea of nature, and, on the practical, by the disappointment of prayer for such blessings and deliverances. This capitulation disguises itself too often under the appearance of religious submission to what is assumed to be a Divinely ordered "course of events," which is supposed to be identical with the direct appointment of the Divine Providence. In reality that "course of events" is only the "closed system" under another name. It is, as a matter of fact, often due mainly to man's indolence, removable ignorance, lust or pride, and is against the pure and loving will of God.

Prayer of the New Testament type, if it sees anything happening, or about to happen, that

macher and Ritschl have all yielded in theory to the old rationalistic metaphysics, and cramped the true liberty of prayer.

is contrary to the Divine Nature as revealed in Jesus Christ, will have no hesitation in asking God to intervene, and, subject to His greater knowledge, in expecting an answer. It will range over the whole sphere of human life, and in all simplicity will ask the Father for all that it needs, in the belief that its petitions make a profound difference to the course of events and to the lives of others. Praying and working are really meant to go together and to supplement each other and assist each other. We have no right to work for anything for which we cannot pray, and we have no right to pray for anything for which we may not work, if our work can do anything to secure its attainment. It may be that our prayers are not heard because God wishes us also to work. It may be that our mere work fails because God wishes us also to pray. In most cases He wills both praying and working.

For what is petitionary prayer but asking God to come to our aid when we are at His work? Countless outward events either help or hinder us in that work. What can be more fatal than to wall off the world of outward events, to forbid prayer within that region, and to confine its influence to the realm of the soul? It is utterly illogical to make this distinction now that we know that psychology has its laws as well as physical nature. Moreover, it, at one sweep, secularises the whole world of outward events for us, when we are really meant to spiritualise every natural and human need, every fact that concerns us, by taking it into the pure atmosphere of prayer, and having it thus associated with the Father in our most inward life.

Petitionary prayer in the fullest sense of the term is every whit as necessary to the full spiritual life as confession and thanksgiving. They are all true and necessary parts of real communion with God.

It is utterly futile, moreover, to expect any sincere man to ask God for any greatly desired good for the sake of praying himself into peace of mind and willingness to do without it. If he cannot rationally expect an answer, he should not go through the farce of praying for it! The assurance may often come to such a man in such prayers that he is in error in asking for some definite good thing, but that, as it were, is a by-product of the prayer. If he come to believe that such by-products are the only results of prayer, a sincere man will stop praying and so he will get neither direct nor indirect results.

I have already pointed out how extraordinarily strong is Christ's language about the power of petitionary prayer. This remains undeniable whether we accept the historicity of His miracles or not. Why do so many modern commentators show themselves nervous and embarrassed when dealing with them? For precisely the same reasons as those for which men reject the historicity of the miracles. There is something in the very intellectual climate of our time that is inimical to such sayings and deeds. I have endeavoured to show what these intellectual hindrances are, but we are concerned here mainly with practical difficulties, and that these are very real I should never think of denying. The truth is that most men and women in our day know little of obvious and striking answers to prayer, any more than they know of miracles.

I think not a few would state their difficulty here in some such terms as these—"Granted that all you have said is true, that the intellectual difficulties to-day are no longer very substantial, and that Jesus Christ had incomparably more faith in the power of prayer than we moderns have,—what do you make of the broad fact that we, all of us, or most of us, have repeatedly had our most earnest prayers apparently refused? We have prayed for the preservation of our young friends from death in battle, and we have lost them; for the recovery of others from illness, and they have died; for success in honest toil for lawful ends, and we have failed; for the opening of the iron doors of circumstance which kept us from attaining our fullest usefulness, and we have been disappointed. What do you make of unanswered prayer?" It is because of this practical difficulty that many have grasped at the idea of a region in which, by its very nature, prayer has, by the appointment of God, no right of way. This is a vain anodyne. Let us test the method. The sharpest trials of faith are those prayers for the spiritual good of ourselves and others that seem unanswered. What are we to make of the apparent failures of intercessory prayer? Why is the spiritual awakening of a community so long delayed, why are there so few conversions of a striking kind? Are we to fall back here again on psychological laws and necessities, indicating that this is another region into which the power of prayer must not intrude? So the scope of prayer is allowed to contract until nothing is left but the narrow sphere of individual, spiritual need. But, one asks, How long will that road remain open? We may rest assured that here, too, the shadow of necessity and law will speedily enter, and that all petitionary prayer will be reduced to auto-suggestion. This whole way of reasoning seems to me radically wrong, and is bound in the end to lead to the disintegration of living, personal religion.

But the practical difficulty remains. What are we to make of it? I would say, first of all, that the difficulty is gravely overstated. There are very many who will bear witness that in their own experience prayer has been answered, and that that answer has by no means been confined to the inner region of the soul, but has been plain and clear in the outward world of events as well. Outward difficulties of circumstances have been surprisingly and inexplicably removed, and deliverances from danger have been experienced, of which the only reasonable explanation that can be given is that they were in answer to prayer. Now be it remembered that if so much as one such answer has ever been actually given, the whole theory of a closed course of events, within which prayer is of no avail, must be abandoned. If the theory gives comfort to some, it is at the expense of declaring that the whole immensely wide and varied story of Divine answers to human prayers, from New Testament days right down through all the Christian ages to our own time, has been one prolonged and persistent hallucination. And this, for any one who knows the literature and history, and has any sympathy with it, is unbelievable. What the history does unmistakably show is that striking answers to prayer in the outward world of events, as well as in the question of spiritual influence upon others, are usually associated with individual men and women of a certain spiritual type characterised by a vivid experience of the Divine presence, and a simple trust in the goodness, the power, and the liberty of God; in other words, by a very strong and simple faith. Outwardly they are often at opposite poles. Imagine St Francis, St Catherine of Sienna, Luther, Fox, Wesley, and George Müller gathered in one room together, and the antagonisms and the shocks that they would impart to each other until they began to confer on the power of prayer, and the unanimity with which on that point they would confront the doubter! There are very many obscure and humble men and women who could bear a like testimony, many of them living among us to-day. With all respect to Modernism of the type we are here thinking of, its theory is too devastatingly simple to account for the complexity of the facts.

But supposing we feel this, and grant that some prayers for outward good, and that some prayers of intercession have been answered, why have so many been apparently unanswered? The ordinary answer to this is simply to confess that we do not know, but that for all that we trust God and believe in the power of prayer. That is a sound and true temper of spirit, and at no stage of knowledge of Divine things can we dispense with it. "God is great and knoweth all things." We know but "the outskirts of His ways." "Clouds and darkness are about Him. Righteousness and justice are the foundations of His throne." That is also our assurance. Nor, as it seems to me, is that simple faith in the moral reason behind all things any whit less rational than that elemental faith in the fundamental rationality and order of the physical universe, which to-day is sustaining thousands of scientific investigators of the unknown in all the laboratories of the civilised world. How often, as these words are being written, are baffled men of science all over the earth strengthening their hearts for new theories, new experiments, new ventures of the tameless reason of man, sustained by simple faith that the difficulties must yield and disclose the hidden order. When that impulse dies, the human intelligence and the human race will die too. Religious men and women should understand it, for they have the key to it in their own quest for moral reason in the great ways of God. But while we hold that faith, we must, like our brothers of science, press on into the unknown, and ask if we can tell why so many prayers remain apparently unanswered. One answer that must rise at once to the lips of all honest men and women must be: "Our prayers were apparently unanswered because it was not good for us that they should be answered. We have proved that in our own experience, since those days when the heavens seemed like brass over our despairing heads. We have learned something by that experience that we could not have done without. Life, it may be, has been barer and darker than it would have been had our prayer been answered, but something has been given instead that we would not give up for all the world, and that bears in it the promise of indefinite retrieval of all that has been lost. The evil has been overruled in part already for good, and will, we believe, in future be completely so overruled."

Such is the answer of faith, and I believe that it is a sound answer. But let us look into it more closely. The prayer, it is said, was unanswered because it was not good for us, and for all, that it should be answered. This is something quite different from mere physical impossibility; it is a personal and a contingent moral necessity, which is not to be toned down to the mere generality that the maintenance of physical law is essential for man's general well-being. The argument is that we were not *morally* ready for such an answer to our prayer as we desired. Why? Now, I submit that on the view of the teaching of the Gospels, which has been taken above, there is a clear answer. There must have been some lack of faith, and of hope, and of love which made us morally immature. "We were not ready for it." Is there not a great unconscious admission here which goes to the very roots of the whole problem of apparently unanswered prayer? Does not the whole attempt to solve that problem, by putting the responsibility for unanswered prayer on the nature of the physical universe and God, assume that we were ready for it, and that our readiness for it was thwarted by something alien and niggardly in our environment? Surely that is making a very great and quite unproved assumption. Do we not instinctively feel in many of our prayers some doubt as to whether this or that particular thing that we greatly desire may really be best? About many particular "good things," though not about all, we surely must be uncertain, unless we claim omniscience, and so we say, in our praying, "if it be Thy Will." What do we really mean by that? Surely we mean "if we," or "if others are ready for it." We have here, in a word, a tacit admission of the whole point at issue that the great promises in prayer are to a large extent conditional upon our being able to make a good spiritual use of them—in other words, that we have a measure of faith, and hope, and love. Conversely, it is not surprising that He who showed these things in supreme measure should have received supreme answers from the Father.

But, coherent and attractive and in line with the whole New Testament teaching about prayer as in many respects this view may seem to be, is there not in it something dangerous and repellent? Do we not purchase the relief to faith in God, which comes from throwing the responsibility of the tragedy of human life on man, too dear? Does it not tend to make prayer a kind of dictation to God? Does not making faith a condition of prevailing prayer introduce the conception of merit into what ought to be a free filial utterance of the human soul, and an implicit submission to Divine wisdom and sovereign power? Does it not add a new and wellnigh intolerable burden to the trial of unanswered prayer to know that it was unanswered because of our own fault? Finally, does not the whole theory tend to weaken our faith in the all-controlling power of God?

First, it is necessary to point out that if these difficulties follow, then they must all have been acutely felt by the first disciples and the first Christian generation. I do not see that there can be any real doubt as to what Christ said about prayer to His disciples and contemporaries. The only question is as to whether we are under the same order as they.

But, in truth, the difficulties seem to rest on some misunderstanding. To begin with, when we say that faith, hope, and love are conditions of prevailing prayer, we do not say that God answers only the prayers of those who have the "faith that moves mountains." He is sovereign love, and in His wisdom and freedom can hear the feeblest prayer from the most sinful soul. It does not impair the promise to the greater faith that God should hear, also, him whose faith is only "as a grain of mustard seed." All generalisations about God's ways must necessarily be incomplete. All that we are here asserting is the positive principle that true faith will always win its answer. But the sovereign Father may of His pure grace and wisdom go beyond this general principle and give great answers even to small faith. Again, to think of faith as meritorious is wholly beside the mark. When a man comes into true filial relations with God, he gets beyond merit altogether. Everything in the new life is of Grace. But Grace has its own laws. If we never think about it or realise it, it will in general have no power over us. If we take time to realise it, it will remould us. But that is not to ascribe merit to thought and realisation, and think of our progress in the spiritual life as reward for our merit. The true relation here is not one of merit and reward, but of cause and consequence, condition and fulfilment, and so is it with faith and prayer.

Further, even though we may choose to set aside the plain teaching of our Lord on this want of faith as one of the great causes of our comparative impotence in prayer, one of the great reasons therefore for the sway of tragedy in human life, is it possible to deny the plain truth that it is our want of love rather than God's will that works countless sorrows in human destiny? We might just as well ascribe these sorrows, also, to the unconditional will of our Father in heaven, as impute to Him the tragedies of unanswered prayer. So, also, is it with hope. How much of the actual "martyrdom of man" is ascribed to the tyranny of nature and circumstance, when in truth its real cause is men's nervelessness, cowardice, and want of that courage of hope which has been the spring of all scientific progress. One must confess that the resolute optimism which keeps science at its countless unsolved problems is a standing rebuke to our religion, and is one of the great reasons why much of the virile intelligence of our day is being withdrawn from religious to scientific thought. Practical optimistic minds instinctively turn to that quarter of the horizon which is fullest of enterprise, energy, and hope. But if these things are true of love and of hope, is it not precisely what we should expect to find that the sovereign powers of prayer should depend upon the faith with which we pray? Can we expect God to verify weak and false conceptions of Himself by striking answers to prayers, which start from cramped conceptions of His power and love and liberty to help men? If it is true that we are to blame for unanswered prayer, by all means let us face the truth. It is the only safe way and the only way worthy of sincere men and women.

It is further very important in understanding the whole matter that we should realise the great influence which the life of the whole community has upon the faith or unbelief of the individual. This, I think, answers the protest that it must add a new burden to life to ascribe unanswered prayer to our own unbelief, but that if we can ascribe it to the natural order or the inscrutable will of God the burden is easier to bear. It is necessary to say here first of all that this last ascription is a dangerous argument to use. Many things of old, many things even in the days of our forefathers, used unquestioningly to be ascribed to God's unconditional will which we now know were due simply to man's own ignorance and indolence. We shall see presently how often, under this fatal obsession, the Christian Church has set itself against "the increasing purpose" of God, and obstructed the path of science, and of political and social progress, and lost for generations the moral leadership that it should have exercised in the great life of the world.

The whole argument is, in truth, too narrowly conceived when we think of it as implying that if a man prays for a thing which he is sure is good and fails to get it, the fault lies solely in himself. We are all, as has been repeatedly urged in this volume, members of society. We are bound to it by countless ties of kinship and sympathy. We partake in its heroisms and share in its apostasies. We experience contagions of faith and unbelief. Thus we have each our own personal life and freedom, and we can, up to a certain point, break clear for good or for evil. When Abraham began the story of faith by going out of Ur of the Chaldees, he at one and the same time acknowledged the fatal power of the unbelieving community to suppress dawning faith, and asserted the power of the individual to break clear of it. The other and the happier side of this power of the community over the individual is that it prevents the latter from falling below a certain level. When a community is inspired by any great emotion to a certain elevation of spirit, all its citizens for the time become heroic. But when it sinks it is, indeed, hard for any individual to rise above it. In general all heroic action in any community has its roots in the common mind. Such actions and the lives which find expression in them are like those islands which are peaks in a submerged ridge of mountains. They seem isolated wonders in the ocean, but in truth they are borne up by a common foundation of rock.

Now if we apply this well-known and generally admitted truth to the matter in hand we may say first of all that the roots of the faith of the Jesus of history lay deep in the historic faith of Israel. How He rose so far above it is His secret. He lifted His disciples and the first Christian age towards His own level, though compared with His their faith was " as a grain of mustard seed." But they were a believing community, and the faith of that community even in " that hard pagan world " enabled its humblest members, as history shows, to live a heroic life, and its greater spirits to expect and to achieve great things by prayer. To-day the common level has fallen, and the whole influence of the society around us, which comes to us along a hundred channels, depresses the spiritual imagination, and contracts the horizon of what is believed possible.

> The world is too much with us, late and soon,
> Getting and spending we lay waste our powers.

To the temptations of worldliness there is added in our day an intellectual fascination by the order of nature, caused by the marvellous progress of science. It is not an age which easily believes in the Divine Transcendence and the expectancy, which a vivid realisation of that Transcendence inspires, that God will do anything beyond the ordinary " course of nature " and events. Therefore, the individual to-day often finds it very hard to maintain his faith in prayer and in the Living God. The contagion of the unbelief of his time paralyses him. Ancestral and subconscious influences are swathed about him and add their restraining might to the suggestions which pour in upon him from the literature, the art, and the thought of his time. In other words, the unbelief whose spell has to be broken is not simply his personal responsibility, but the corporate unbelief of his time, from which he is the vicarious sufferer. It is this spiritual solidarity of mankind which makes the existence of the Christian Church so vital a necessity for the life of the Christian man or woman. It may, indeed, be argued that our Lord's promises to faith and the Charismata to the early Church which were their fulfilment, were given to the Church as a whole rather than to individuals, and that in the present broken and depressed condition of the Church they are meantime in abeyance. I should not question this so long as we remember that it is the Church as a society of believing men and women that is meant, and not merely a Church orthodox in doctrine or order, or both. The promises of the Gospels are always to faith, whether it be "corporate" or individual. The awakening of the Church can only begin with the individual, but the individual can only reach his true stature through the society. Certainly, if the Church were nearly all that it ought to be, we should see the result of the life of prayer in the life of the individual in a way and on a scale that we rarely witness. So, in the first Christian ages the vitality of the corporate faith of the Church lifted its members above the torpor of the pagan world. So, to-day individuals, as has always been the way, break clear from the carnal level, and when they appear, strange and wonderful things happen. The dull world echoes and rings as it did of old, and the roll of heroes of faith begun in the eleventh chapter of Hebrews is continued.

Such pioneers of faith, going right back to the

Jesus of history, one and all start from a richer conception of God than their contemporaries, and He still verifies that conception. May we not say that He only awaits to-day richer and freer conceptions of Himself, of His sovereign reality, power and love and liberty to help men? Such, at least, seems to me to be the plain meaning of our Lord's own teaching about faith.

But, finally, does not the view set forth in this volume exclude acceptance and resignation, such as our Lord showed in His prayer in the Garden, when, after repeated prayer that the cup might pass from Him, He said, "Nevertheless, not my will but Thine be done"? How are we to combine resignation to evil with revolt against evil, submissive with rebellious faith? To-day when men think of faith, they instinctively, I believe, think mainly of submissive, acquiescent faith. I fear that the great majority of people, when they pray the Lord's Prayer, interpret the clause "Thy will be done" as expressing a believing acceptance of the inevitable. Yet in the context it can hardly mean that. It comes after petitions for the fuller revelation of the name that expresses the nature of God as Father, and for the coming of the Kingdom. "We have turned,"[2] it has been truly said, "what was meant to be a battle-cry into a wailing litany." That is symptomatic of the religious temper of our time. What seems empirically inevitable is regarded without more ado as "the will of God."

I fear that that springs not so much from a deepening of faith as from a weakening of the idea of God.

[2] By Archbishop Temple.

Yet we have here undoubtedly, in the moment of the agony at the very climax of a life of heroic, rebellious faith, the note of acceptance and submission, and it reminds us that at any moment the Christian must be prepared to carry the cross after his Master and "fill up that which remaineth of the sufferings of Christ."

The story, as we have it in St Matthew, is of a threefold prayer in the Garden for the passing of the cup, with submission to the Sovereign Will of the Father. Then comes the announcement to the disciples and the coming of the hour, the kiss of Judas, and the apprehension. A disciple draws his sword and Christ bids him sheathe it, and tells him that, if He chose, He could have more than twelve legions of angels coming to His support. This last remarkable saying is peculiar to St Matthew's narrative, but all the three narratives make Christ warn His disciples against "temptation,"[3] which seems to imply that He has Himself just passed through and overcome it. Then He gives Himself up, and with the faith of acceptance passes on to a freely chosen death.

I think that the plain meaning of the whole Gospel story is that the faith of Jesus was in the main a creative faith by virtue of which He was continually militant against the whole dark realm of sin and suffering and tragedy, "the Kingdom of the evil one" of contemporary belief, and continually seeking to bring in a better world in its place. This was

[3] Possibly a reference back to the first temptation in the wilderness, when Satan tempted Him to use the heavenly power amiss.

His normal attitude of mind, and is meant to be the normal temper of His disciples, who are sustained in this by their confidence in the power and love of the Father. But there came to Him an assurance that the end for which He laboured, the complete overthrow of sin and tragedy, men being what they were, could be better secured under the vicarious law by His going through the way of the Cross, and He deliberately ceased to pray for deliverance, and though He might have had it, trusted the overruling Will of the Father and went on to His death, as a freely chosen lot. His prayer was not, according to the text of the Gospels, refused. How could it have been refused, when immediately afterwards He says that supernatural powers would have delivered Him, if He had so chosen. We have, therefore, no record that any prayer of Jesus was ever refused. Indeed, in a singular passage which can only be explained as a reference to the prayer in the Garden, the writer of the Epistle to the Hebrews seems to say explicitly that it was answered. But He ceased to ask it. He asked, instead, that the Father's will should be done. That does not mean that the Cross in itself was that Will. The Cross was an abomination, hateful then and always to God. But the Cross being historically there, it was God's Will that He should face and triumph over it, and, when He saw the real issues, this became His will too, and He prayed for the power to consummate them, and so by enduring the Cross destroy the cross, and all that world of inhumanity of which it was the symbol.

Now, how are we to translate all this into Christian practice ? We are to go into the age-long war against all sin and all tragedy of circumstance as well in firm faith that our Father wills to make an end of them all. That, alone, is the full Christian idea of God, which sets the standard for all Christian living and prayer. We are, therefore, to wage a truceless war against everything which corrupts the soul, and ruins the body and mind, and kills the liberty of man. We are to carry on this war by creative and rebellious faith, rebellious not against the Supreme Will but against the intruding and transient evils of human life.

But if by our own failure of faith, of love, and of hope, or by the vicarious law, we fall in the battle, we are to carry that battle as far into the ranks of the enemy as we can, to win the last inch of ground, and, in falling, to commit the unfinished battle to the Captain, who in the end will bring it to complete victory.

> Let the victors when they come,
> When the forts of folly fall,
> Find thy body by the wall.

It may be that He will tell us that the cause needs our apparent defeat. But until He reveals that to us we have no right to abandon the struggle, and succumb to the powers of darkness, however overwhelming they may seem to be.

But, finally, does not the whole theory of the contingent character of the tragic element in human experience, which ascribes it in so great a measure to the shortcomings and sins of men, fatally weaken that faith in the sovereign power of God, which lies at the very foundations of every true Christian life? This is the most fundamental of all the difficulties.

It is stated with great force by Mr Donald Baillie in his recently published volume on *Faith in God*.[4] He is in general sympathy with the view of the power of faith and the nature of outward evil taken by Miss Dougall, and in a greater or less degree by the "Cumnor group" of theologians, and recognises the importance of its contribution to a better understanding of the Gospel narratives. But he feels acutely the danger of taking this as a complete account of the Divine government in relation to the outward evil of the world. The religious nature, he believes, demands that we should believe that everything that concerns us is under Divine control. The believing man must believe that all things that touch him are in God's hands. But then if they are real evils, how can they be Divine appointments? He finds here a real paradox, and believes that we shall only be able to do justice to the still dimly understood reality by holding fast to both its terms.

We have here, obviously, an old difficulty coming up under new forms, the difficulty which divided Augustinianism and Pelagianism in the early centuries, and Calvinism and Arminianism after the Reformation, and which appears to-day in philosophical regions between the Absolutist philosophy and those who believe in a limited God. I think that Mr Baillie's criticisms are in the main directed against an extremer view of the outward evils in

[4] This notable book only came into my hands when the whole of the earlier part of this volume was already in print, or I should gladly have availed myself of its aid to a much fuller degree than has been possible. It is a contribution of uncommon value to the present state of the question.

human life than I should hold, or than I think is necessary for the position maintained in this volume. I agree with him not only that God has ordained the world-order, by ignorance and misuse of which sickness, calamity, and death befall the children of men, and discipline them out of wrong ways of thinking and living, but I believe that over and above this He can so overrule evil that it works out supreme good. The Cross is there in history as the final proof of that.

In itself it is the sum of all human infamies. It originated in the very slums of the human heart, for it is the expression of cruelty, and of contempt for human nature. There ought never to have been a cross, as there ought never to have been stakes and racks and thumb-screws. The story of the Crucifixion, also, is a shame to Israel and Rome alike. Even the disciples of Jesus make a poor show in history at this point beside the disciples of Socrates. Yet God has so overruled it that it is the sublimest manifestation of Himself in human history, the living heart of all its higher progress. The Cross of Calvary has, in fact, destroyed crucifixion in all civilised lands.

It is thus, further, the supreme fact in human history which demonstrates that all sin and all tragedy are retrievable. It proves that Love is mightier than hatred, as the Resurrection proves that Life is greater than Death. Taken together, they are the Divine assurance to mankind of the final triumph of good over evil, of the goodness and the omnipotence of God, for what God has done with this Cross He can do with all the crosses of all His children.

CHAPTER VIII

THE FAITH OF JESUS

THE question will at this point, no doubt, be asked, "Whither does your argument tend?" Does not the endeavour to make the miracles of Jesus part of the substance instead of the accidents of the Christian faith unduly complicate matters and lay an unnecessary burden on that faith in so difficult a time as our own? Have we not by the singular grace of God to our generation recovered the Jesus of history, and a simplified faith in the Fatherhood of God and the brotherhood of man which is easy to believe and which yields a sufficient light for daily life? I should be disposed to say, in reply to this, that I share with those who feel the extraordinary value of the recovery of the Jesus of history. This is one of the greatest spiritual events in the story of Christianity and is working as a potent leaven both in the thought and life of our age.

But there are two things that make it impossible for many of us to-day to be satisfied with this simplified version of Christianity. In the first place, it is precisely the use of historical methods in the study of the personality and teaching of Jesus that has compelled us to see that there is something in His teachings about the power of faith and of prayer that is not to-day finding any adequate expression in our current theology and religion, and that the simplified version, which tones them down to something little better than commonplaces about the power of a hopeful and courageous disposition in practical Christian endeavour, is anything but true to fair historical methods of interpretation. To reduce the plain meaning of such sayings in this way is to impose our modern limitations upon something of primitive genius and inspiration.

Secondly, we have a further difficulty. We whole-heartedly agree with all that is said about the immeasurable gain to religion of the re-discovery of the historical Jesus, and the humanising and deepening of the idea of God which has come with the realising of His universal Fatherhood. But we find it impossible to silence the question that immediately arises from that very deepening of our thoughts of "the Father." Why does Nature often seem so appallingly unfatherly? Under the old Jewish faith in "the great and terrible God," or under the God of the Schoolmen, or the Sovereign Lord of Calvin, or the great First Cause of the rationalist, the problem is not nearly so acute. But why do such things happen in the realm of the Father, "the God and Father of our Lord Jesus Christ"? In a word, the recovery of the earliest revelation of God as the universal Father has sharpened the edge of the master problem of Theism, the problem of evil. The more full of light the revelation is shown to be, the more sharply stand out the sinister and tragic elements in human destiny, and the more strange seems to be the martyrdom of man. It is as if each new and deeper affirmation about God awoke a new and stronger denial from the unexhausted antagonist. Some minds do not seem to feel this difficulty. It is mainly to these, I think, that the simplified Humanitarian conception of the personality of Jesus appeals most strongly. They do not feel deeply the unexplained and apparently sinister side of Nature's dealings with man, which made the Jews of our Lord's time think of the tragic element in the world as due to the power of the Evil One, and which, as we have seen, led to such passionate protests against Nature from some of the most penetrating thinkers of our time.

We have already shown that on a sufficiently wide view of Nature, and of her total reaction on mankind, these pessimistic estimates of Nature lose much of their power, for historically we owe the very ethical standards by which we condemn Nature to the hard discipline to which she has subjected mankind. But does this widening of our view of Nature, which makes her the foster-mother of the intellectual and moral development of the human race, carry us all the way in explaining her remorseless and sinister side? I confess that to me it does not go quite so far. It goes a long way, but it does not go the whole way. It makes a very great deal of the human tragedy removable and therefore educative. We can see that if men grow in loyalty to each other, in love, in the sense of honour, in strength and courage, and the social virtues generally, then a very great many of the evils to which mankind are at present subject from

Nature will disappear. So, too, with the expansion of Science, man's sovereignty over the dark material forces must still further force back the realm of suffering and darkness. But few are those who believe that the utmost advance of ethical development and intellectual growth can ever abolish the tragic element in human destiny. That is to say, they practically all admit that there is at last an unconditionally fixed and fated element of the tragic in man's lot, an irremovable element of evil inherent in the earthly conditions of human life.

I think I should admit this, so long as we think of man as being purely an ethical and intellectual being. I cannot conceive of the utmost growth in the purely social virtues or the utmost extension, say, of physical science ever giving men that power over all physical limitations, which work suffering, evil, and death. But if man is capable of fuller growth than can be comprised under the words "moral and intellectual progress," if he is capable of coming into the fullest harmony of spiritual communion with the stupendous Being who is sovereign over all the material world, I see no coherent reason for not believing that all tragedy whatsoever is removable from his life, that he may not grow through fellowship with the Sovereign Father of All into complete mastery over all that chains and maims the immortal spirit.

If that, indeed, be the case, then all outward evils whatsoever are removable, and all alike fall into one great system of Divine education of the human race. It is, indeed, difficult to think of any system as being a system of education unless its penalties are removable by the growing teachableness and fidelity of the pupil. Therefore if human experience is really an education of mankind, it would seem to require this conception of the removability of all evil whatever, in order to complete it.

If this be sound reasoning, then it is clear that we must not only look upon Nature as man's educator in science and in morality, but also in religion. Her purpose must not only be to elicit intelligence and the great social virtues, but her ultimate and consummating purpose must be to drive him to God, and to teach him faith, faith in God's power, God's holy love, and God's perfect liberty to help him. In other words, the whole history of man's religion, as well as his moral and intellectual development, has behind it the sublime and austere background of Nature.

Cardinal Newman has given noble expression to this thought of the necessity of Nature as meant to drive men not only into fellowship with each other, but into the beginnings of communion with God. Man, he says, "is permitted much" in the way of controlling "brute mischiefs" of Nature. But there is a reserved region into which he cannot enter, the region of "the Elements."

> But o'er the Elements
> One Hand alone,
> One Hand has sway.
> What influence day by day
> In straiter belt prevents
> The impious Ocean, thrown

Alternate o'er the ever sounding shore?
Or who has eyes to trace
How the Plague came,
Forerun the doublings of the Tempest's pace?
Or the Air's weight and flame
On a set scale explore?
Thus God has willed
That man, when fully skilled
Still gropes in twilight dim;
Encompassed all his hours
By fearfullest powers
Inflexible to him,
That so he may discern
His feebleness,
And e'en for earth's success
To Him in wisdom turn
Who holds for us the keys of either home,
Earth and the world to come.

The austerity of Nature is thus the foster-mother not only of the ethical virtues and of knowledge, but of the prayer of faith, faith in the unseen Reality and Power, as able and free and willing to help the suppliant to escape from or to master the destroying powers of Nature, and to give him that life which God Himself possesses by inherent right. The history of religion shows quite clearly that it is in its historic roots, as Sabatier has said, essentially "a prayer for life," a prayer which becomes wider and expands into communion with God as it develops, but which never loses this fundamental character. It reveals, also, that always in this prayer, inspiring and sustaining it, there is this vital thing, faith, conviction as to the reality and the friendliness of the unseen world. No one would ever pray unless he thought it worth while to pray.

To believe that it is worth while to pray means faith in the ultimate nature of things.

We now turn from these general considerations to determine what Jesus Christ believed about faith, and what is implied in that for His revelation of God.

We have seen in an earlier chapter how great was the position of faith in the religion of the Old Covenant. As Prof. A. B. Davidson has said, faith to the Hebrew was the fundamental virtue. But this discloses itself to the reader only when one looks for it, and discovers it under varying synonyms and parts of speech. So much is this the case that some scholars have maintained that there is surprisingly little about faith in the Old Testament. But when one turns to the Apostolic and sub-Apostolic literature there can be no question of their absorption in the importance of faith, or the all-determining place that it has in their thoughts. For any reference to faith [1] and its two synonyms, belief and trust, in the Old Testament, there are thrice as many in the New, as a reference to any good concordance will show, and when one remembers that the Old Testament is about thrice the length of the New, this, rough as is such a test, is full of meaning.

St Paul's writings, of course, afford the most conspicuous examples of this in the Apostolic writings. To him faith is the great fundamental human virtue, the indispensable condition of all salvation and life and blessing. The references which prove this will be found in an Appendix. They are so

[1] Verbal or substantival.

numerous that to give them here in the text would gravely overload the argument. "It is beyond doubt," says Titius,[2] "that for Paul the Christian life in its beginning and throughout its progress, in things great and in things small, is borne up by faith. This is true not only of the religious functions in the narrower sense, but of the moral functions also." From writings of the New Testament, slightly later and coloured by Alexandrine thought, we need take only one instance.

So deeply persuaded is the writer of the Epistle to the Hebrews of the central and vital place of faith in the spiritual life that, in what is perhaps the deepest and truest account of the Old Testament religion ever committed to writing, he goes through the long roll of its heroes and saints and finds faith the vital and characteristic virtue in them all. It is that in them which made them what they were and enabled them to do what they did, and by virtue of which they have written their names for ever in history, and made it easier for all other men to believe in the unseen world and in God.

Now while this is, I believe, absolutely true of these heroes, it is none the less also true that you get in the Old Testament itself nothing like this explicit and sweeping estimate of faith common both to St Paul and the author of the Epistle to the Hebrews. Where did the New Testament writers get this new insight into the all-important character of faith? Something has happened in the interval which has deepened their whole sense of

[2] *Paulinismus*, p. 214.

the value of faith. There cannot really be any doubt as to where these writers got this new and vital emphasis. They got it straight from Jesus of Nazareth. Indeed the writer of the Epistle to the Hebrews leaves us in no doubt whatever as to this. In the verses which immediately follow the roll of heroes in the eleventh chapter, he speaks of Jesus as "the author" and the "perfecter" of faith. The force of this passage is weakened in our Authorised Version by the gratuitous insertion of "our" before "faith," but this seems to me, clearly, a mistake.

The obvious meaning of this expression is that great as the faith of these heroes was, it was as nothing in comparison with the faith of Jesus. He was its real author, its real beginner. They were like stars that died out in that sunrise of real faith which men saw in Christ. The writer has probably in his mind here the words of Christ Himself when the apostles said to Him, "Lord, increase our faith!" "If ye have faith as a grain of mustard seed, ye shall say unto this mountain, Be thou taken up and removed hence, and it shall obey you." We have the same thought in the Epistle to the Hebrews freely reproduced in the writer's own noble fashion. As compared with Jesus, the heroes had faith only like a grain of mustard seed!

When we turn to the Gospels the secret of this great development in the mind of the apostles as to the sovereign importance of faith becomes, as I have said, perfectly clear.

It is due to the profound impact which the personality, the deeds, and the teaching of Jesus have made upon the whole Apostolic age. I need not repeat what has been said in an earlier chapter about Christ's constant call for faith in God. A reference back to that chapter will show that in effect Jesus said to the men of His land and time, "I have brought the Kingdom of God and all its blessings within your reach. It is for you to take it by faith." He welcomed all such adventurous faith as rose up within men's hearts in answer to His challenge, however crude and undisciplined that faith might seem to be, provided it did not presumptuously seek to use physical violence. But He who forbade this, seems to have preferred vehement faith to mere prudence.

Harnack has, I think, established that this is the meaning of the difficult passage: "From the days of John the Baptist even until now the Kingdom of God is preached and violent men are entering into it." As we have seen, all through His ministry He is continually inciting and encouraging faith, and towards the end, when the shadows of the approaching sacrifice are gathering around Him, the one doubt that seems ever to have crossed His mind as to the certainty of His approaching victory, is as to whether, even when He returns in glory and power, there will be faith enough in the earth for men to take what is brought.

Surely when we sum up what He says about the blessings of the Kingdom, and the need for faith, we have precisely the same emphasis as in St Paul and in the Epistle to the Hebrews. In the Gospels the blessings of the Kingdom are the filial life in God, the hearing and answering of the prayer of faith, and the glory of the life to come. In St Paul we have the same things expressed in terms of his rabbinical training in analogies borrowed from the life of his time—justification, adoption, sanctification, and the manifestations of the Spirit, gifts or "charismata" of "prophecy," "healing," "miracles"—the potent influences that had come into the life of the Church with Pentecost, and, finally, the blessedness of life in the coming æon, when sin and death should be finally broken. All come from God by faith. In all this he is a true disciple of Jesus, who is the unquestionable historical "author" or "pioneer" and "perfection" of faith.

Turning again to the Gospel narrative, we find Christ's call for faith on one and all around Him so constant that one cannot but feel that if He were here in the body in the world once more, and we all gathered round Him, and each of us told Him in turn the story of our failures and tragedies and sins, He would say to each of us: "What has been wrong with you, and what is wrong with you still, is that as yet you have not enough faith in God. You think that the trouble has been due to your indolence, your hatred, and your pride. It may be, but there is something deeper. You must have more faith in God. If you realise that, all evil and tragic things will lose their power."

Now, it may be said, this diagnosis may be true,

but does it really help us? Is there not something even discouraging in His call for faith as the one thing primarily needful? We may discipline our anger, and mortify our pride, and suppress our fleshly thoughts, but who can create faith?

But surely if we look deeper there is something profoundly heartening for humanity here, an implicit assurance about God and the ultimate nature of things of the most sweeping kind.

If a father standing on the frozen waters of a lake encourages his timid child to come on the ice beside him, telling him to trust it, and that there need be no fear, is he not putting the whole force of his personality into telling him something about the ice?

It is quite clear that the whole teaching of Jesus Christ about God, expressed alike in His words and in the whole fashion and mould of His character, implies that God is always nearer, mightier, more loving, and more free to help every one of us than any one of us ever realises. This alone is what makes His incessant summons to faith, and to more faith, coherent and reasonable. This, again, seems to me to imply that mankind generally is under a kind of hypnotic spell about God, which is always contracting and chilling their thoughts of Him, and leading to all kinds of depressing and terrifying illusions about Him. The story of the growth of the disciples' faith is the story of the breaking of that evil spell. If we transport ourselves in imagination into the little company of His disciples, it is not difficult to imagine what the effect upon them of His continual demand for faith in God must have been. Taken along with His own unbroken confidence of God's presence, power, and love, He must have seemed like one holding a continued dialogue with the Unseen One. Yet a doubt must have sometimes crept in. Was it not rather a monologue? No man but He heard the other Voice. We know what to think of men who hold long monologues, talking to people who are not there! Was He mad? The men who sat in the seat of authority, the wise and prosperous and devout, said He was. "He hath an evil spirit!" The issue, as He meant that it should, gradually became inevitable. Either He was a dreamer, or they and all other men were dreamers, walking in the darkness and deeming it to be light. Was He mad about God, thinking Him real, near, mighty beyond imagining, loving beyond hope, when really He was far away in His Heaven, terrible in His justice, and with difficulty restraining His anger? Or were they and all the world mad about God?

Such I doubt not was the early struggle of faith. The issue does not seem to me vitally different to-day. Either Jesus Christ was a dreamer about God, or we are all together dreamers, unbelievers and Christians alike. The difference is only one of degree. We are all alike wrapped in the great earth dream, and He alone was fully awake of all the sons of men; or we men and women of the twentieth century are broad awake to the reality, and He was dreaming His solitary dream. Nothing is more certain than this, that in His teaching about faith in God, and in His practice of it, Jesus was absolutely unique among all the great leaders of religion that history has known. The science of religion has established this once for all. We know more or less exactly what all the acknowledged greatest have taught—the Chinese sages, Gautama, Socrates, Mohammed. In the midst of them stands this figure with His unique and immovable confidence in the Father, His faith that God is always nearer, mightier, more loving, and more free to help every one of us than any one of us ever realises, and that therefore our supreme duty is faith in Him, and the staking of everything we have upon Him, and His purpose of good for mankind. Christianity is this or it is nothing at all. Everything turned then and everything turns still on whether on this central matter Jesus was a dreamer, or the only human being broad awake to the eternal, in such a fashion that if we would come into touch with ultimate Reality we, too, have to follow Him. No other option indeed in such a case is open to us, for not only has none of the great leaders of religion said such things of God in the past, but no one is saying them to-day, except such as, whether they know it or not, are His disciples. This is still His solitary and peculiar teaching about God, the very core and essence of His Revelation.

The first disciples, I take it, must for a time have wavered between the two worlds, the old sane Jewish world of thought as it must have seemed to them, and this new, startling, fascinating, and glorious Presence of the Divine that was breaking in upon them, at first a dreamlike vision of Beauty and then taking to itself, more and more, the firm outlines of Reality and making the old Jewish thoughts in turn dreamlike. As St Paul put it, the first Christians " saw the glory of God in the face of Jesus Christ." I remember that many years ago I was at a long concert of classical music, and not having any adequate understanding of its greatness, I was feeling rather weary of it, and my attention was wandering, when my eye fell on the face of a man sitting near me. I was startled, for his face was transfigured as by an interior light, and his eyes were shining. He seemed like one carried beyond all fear and care and sorrow. It was quite impossible for me to doubt that he was hearing things I could not hear, and seeing things I could not see. I saw the " light of the knowledge of the glory " of music on his face, so that for the moment I could see that it was, though I could not hear what it was. Something like this was the first Christian experience, and it has remained the standard ever since. The typical Christian name for the Supreme Being is, it has been truly said by Ritschl, " the God and Father of our Lord Jesus Christ," and so unique was the vision and the experience even to a Hebrew, that, as we have seen, the writer of the Epistle to the Hebrews can say that Jesus was to him, the beginner and the perfection of faith. The power of the personality of Jesus was so great that, working through the disciples, it broke the hypnotic spell of unbelief and swept the whole first Christian generation, the generation that wrote the New Testament and reared the Christian Church into something of His own faith in God, and so perpetuated the seed of it in the world.

What makes this immovable confidence of Jesus in God so profoundly reassuring is the other great marvel of His personality,—His profound sense of the sacredness of man. There have been not a few among the heroes and even among the saints of faith of whom we must admit that this cannot be said. We feel that such God-intoxicated men and women have been so absorbed in the Divine glory that they seem to have had too little sense of the pathos of human life, its cruel mysteries, the haunting "sense of tears in mortal things." Their very zeal for God has made them sometimes, we feel, unduly hard upon men. What are we to make of the saints who condoned and even encouraged persecution, and the theologians who have given us great thoughts of the Divine purpose, "deep as the grave, high as the Eternal throne," but have combined them sometimes with inhuman thoughts of men?

Something of Christianity was surely lacking there, which makes us feel that they never adequately felt the real anguish of the unsolved "riddle of the painful earth," and the shadow that it seems to cast on the face of God. But we cannot say this of the Crucified. He has taught us all humanity, just as He has taught us faith. From Him the modern world has learned the secret of that "enthusiasm of humanity," which is the very leaven of all that is finest and best in our civilisation. Yet He who kindled this fire of the enthusiasm of humanity is the same who has taught us, and who to-day above all others stands for unbounded confidence in Him who ordained the whole tremendous system of discipline under which all men live and suffer and die.

Their compassion for suffering humanity has driven not a few in our day into rebellion against "the Cosmic order," and denial of a conscious, loving, and Almighty Creator and Sovereign, who has ordained, it would appear, "the martyrdom of man." That this is one of the tensions in the mind of our own age, is manifest not only in the philosophical writers quoted at length in an earlier chapter, but in the works of a great artist like Thomas Hardy, the secret of whose pessimism I take to be that he strove to combine the Christian valuation of man with the negation of the Christian view of the cosmic order, and made a futile attempt to derive human reason, nobility, and piety from a Being who is in effect lower and meaner than man. How could Hardy's mocking "President of the Immortals" ever have created human beings like Tess and Gabriel? How could the Unconscious Mind ever blindly work its way out to the "all things fair" that the author of *The Dynasts* hoped for? With Lord Bacon we may surely say that we "could sooner believe all the fables of the Alcoran." There must be a more reasonable account of a cosmos that every true man of science believes to be greater and more full of order than he has discovered, every great painter knows to be lovelier than he has painted, and every great poet knows to be nobler than he ever sang. Is it not all in perfect conformity with this inner conviction of thinker and artist alike that God must be mightier and more loving and readier to help us all than any one of us has ever realised, and that Jesus should put at the centre of His message the call to unbounded faith?

The solution of Jesus is that the Absolute is so much greater and better and fairer than we are that we cannot as yet fully understand Him, but none the less can go beyond our knowledge by faith, just as genius continually wings its way beyond demonstration, showing the road that the slower-footed understanding must follow. He Himself is embodied Faith and so becomes embodied Revelation. The glory of God shines through Him, and the Universe responds and reveals its hidden depth and meaning in His life and deeds and death and resurrection. Thereby a way is broken through the dense cloud of unbelief for the coming of His Spirit.

The faith of Jesus in the Almighty Father, like all faith, is woven of three strands—faith in God's power and reality, faith in His love, and faith in His perfect liberty to help men.

(1) The first is the primitive thing in all religion: "Power belongeth unto God." Whatever weakens this primitive thing in religion weakens faith. In the very nature of the case Religion conceives of this Power as power over the world. This excludes the identification of God and the world, for all real religion appeals to God against the immediately threatening or tempting world. We may use the term the Supreme Reality instead of the term the Supreme Power, because it conveys even more strongly the sense of superiority over the world of appearance. Compared with God

the world is a vanishing mist, but it is not a mist that He cannot control. Some may feel that there is something lacking in the words "appearance" and "reality" as descriptive of the world and God. Control is certainly essential to the religious conception of their relation.[4] It appears to me that Jesus had a unique awareness of the reality and power of God and that He was able to communicate this in a unique degree. With most of us the real plague is "the seeming unreality of the spiritual life." The world to-day is so urgent and so interesting that we can hardly help conceding reality to it in the full sense, and giving only what remains of our energy and thought to God. There is a curious and pathetic passage in one of William James's letters in which, in reply to a questionnaire, he says that for himself he has no immediate sense of the Divine Reality, but that he recognises that other men, and notably the great mystics, have it, and that he believes their testimony. I think this is to-day a very common experience. Again, even when men have this "open vision" it fluctuates. Great experiences of danger and great scenes in nature suddenly call it forth. I remember one friend telling me that sometimes in the acutest dangers of the war an almost physical sense of the reality and power of God came to him and drove away all fear. The brother of another, travelling alone by night to London on the way to the front, experienced, as the hours went by, an ever-deepen-

[4] Professor Hogg shows how the Idealist conception of appearance and reality may be combined with the Christian conception of the miraculous. *Redemption from this World*, ch. v., and pp. 262-5.

ing sense of the presence of God, which changed the whole course of his life. Yet another once described to me how, in rock climbing in a remote and sterile region in the north-west of Scotland, his companion was suddenly killed beside him, and how in the vast and wonderful mountain solitude around him, as he stood beside the shattered body far from human aid, the whole scene became suddenly full of the Divine Presence. If such experiences are truthful, their only possible explanation is that something that blinds us has been taken away.

Most of us have direct or indirect experiences of this kind in our memories. They do not seem to us hallucinations. Rather do we recognise them as moments of awakening to what is always there. Always there is that sense of Power, Sovereignty, and Reality as an essential part of the experience.

Now it is impossible to study the personality of Jesus without seeing that this awareness of God was part of the very substance of His daily life. What is momentary and transient with most of us, was for Him unbroken. It comes out in His words. "God is to Him the Almighty Presence and Reality. In opposition to the Almighty power, man simply does not count for anything. And more must be said. Not only in the domain of ethical and religious life is God the only Mighty One. The same is true in the physical Universe. The world signifies nothing, God alone signifies everything." [5]

Even more strikingly does it come out in His actions. Take, for instance, the story of His

[5] Titius, *Die Neutestamentliche Lehre von der Seligkeit*, vol. I. *Jesu Lehre vom Reiche Gottes*, pp. 108-109.

raising the daughter of Jairus. He is making His way through the crowd with the father, when the messengers meet them with the fatal words—"Thy daughter is dead, why troublest thou the Master any further?" One may safely say that every other human being in history would have taken that word "dead" as final, and turned back. Nobody would have blamed Him if He had done so, and He risked His whole reputation by going on. Yet He went on. What was death in comparison with God? That lets us see deep into His spirit. The going on is every whit as unique as the wonder which followed. The unique quality of His religious life explains the unique event which followed.

I have said that this profound sense of the Reality and Power of God is the fundamental thing in all religion whatever. The note of the Sovereign Power of God resounds through the whole Old Testament and finds its richest expression there in those sayings about His omnipotence, omnipresence, omniscience, and eternity, of which the literature of the Old Covenant is so full. Theism, as Tiele has truly remarked, can never compromise on this point of the Divine omnipotence without losing half its power. We must, of course, distinguish here between true and false ideas of omnipotence. God may limit Himself by creating free human spirits. It is difficult indeed to see how He could be really omnipotent if He could not create what He pleased. But it is inconceivable that He can be limited by any independent and rival power. This is fundamental to the whole mind of Jesus, and is an essential element in His faith.

(2) But it would be quite conceivable that if this profound sense of the Sovereign Reality of God stood alone, the possession of it might be a curse instead of a blessing and emancipation to men. The "seeming unreality" of God may in fact be a condition of man's preserving his sanity until he wins such confidence in the love of God that He is not only able to bear, but to exult in the sense of His Sovereign Reality. So we come to the second strand of the threefold cord of Faith, the Love of God.

Jesus Christ reveals this by His teaching, by His signs, by His whole personality, and supremely by His Cross. His seizing upon the relationship of fatherhood as yielding the truest name for God, and His assertion, "If ye then being evil know how to give good gifts to your children, how much more shall your Heavenly Father give the Holy Spirit to them that ask Him," at once give us an enduring symbol of the Divine Nature, and the assurance that the Reality excels the symbol.

Further, His own filial personality mediates to us by its incomparable human sympathy more perfectly than words can do, the very heart of the unseen Father.

Yet again the "miracles" are surely part of that revelation. They show us how we are to think of the Divine Love and Pity, which cares not only for the souls of men, but for their bodies. They show us that we are to think of the Divine Love in the simplest way as delighting in the dispelling of pain, the restoring of sanity, the satisfying of hunger, the preservation of life, the dispelling of premature death, just the things which ordinary human love glories in being able to do. But supreme sacrifice is the most convincing thing of all, when it is freely chosen for love's sake. So by teaching, by living in converse with His fellows, by His signs, and by His Cross, Jesus reveals that the Supreme Reality is the Supreme Loving Kindness, so that they who receive the revelation know the awakening of Faith.

(3) But all would have been of little avail unless there had gone along with faith in God's Sovereign Reality and His Fatherly Love faith in His perfect Liberty to help men, His power to intervene in the ordinary course of events, to act creatively whenever the real spiritual interest of His children requires it. The weakening of this is, perhaps, what to-day hampers Faith more than any other cause. The shadow of the "closed system" falls upon prayer, obsesses men's imagination and limits their hopes. The world becomes rigid. The glove of silk becomes a glove of stone.

Now it is perfectly clear from all the Gospel narratives that Jesus Christ had no such chilling shadow upon His faith in God. One of His best modern interpreters has put the matter here decisively. Jesus, he of course admits, knew nothing of our modern science. But even if He had, it would not have made the least difference to Him in this regard. As it was He had a definite idea of the course of nature. "He knows about seed-time and harvest, and the rules of the weather; He knows the need of preparation for the building of houses and vineyard towers, as for the waging of war; He knows all this and gives it its due place, and even praises the unfaithful steward for his cleverness. Yet, nevertheless, His summons to trust in God and prayer sounds as absolute as if there were no such thing as prudence and human toil. In the miracle-working faith this thoroughgoing and universal way of looking at things comes to the point in the sharpest way. The world of Nature is, in comparison with God, nothing, and He alone is the Almighty Lord."[6]

I do not think that there can be any doubt that this is a true account of the faith of Jesus. It was an essential part of His response to the Sovereignty of God. He believed, as I have said, in His perfect liberty to help men, a truth which was obscured so long as men believed in the completeness of the scientific explanation of reality, but whose possibility is now in process of being demonstrated by our fuller knowledge of the limits of science.

[6] Titius, *Jesu Lehre vom Reiche Gottes*, p. 109.

CHAPTER IX

THE PROBLEM OF EVIL

It has been said in a preceding chapter that when we speak of faith in God to-day what is usually meant is trustful acquiescence in the course of events. That this is a large part of the life of faith is undoubtedly true. The prayer of Jesus in Gethsemane, " Father, not my will but Thine be done," is a clear proof that it was part of the faith of Jesus. But by far the larger number of references to faith in His teaching are of an apparently very different kind. The faith to which they call us is to anything rather than acquiescence, it is rather to uncompromising rebellion against what seems the natural course of events. Men are encouraged to seek deliverance from diseases incurable by the medical science of their day, from maladies that by long neglect have become chronic, from premature death, and even from the untamed forces of nature itself. What are we moderns to make of such an astonishing saying as this: " Have faith in God, for verily I say unto you that if ye have faith as a grain of mustard seed ye shall say to this mountain, Be thou removed hence, and it shall obey you ! " No doubt, as I have said, this is metaphorical language. But Christ certainly meant something more wonderful than what He had done just before He said it. When taken in its whole context it means something very drastic, and quite unmodern. I take it that it can only mean, that if a disciple of Jesus sees any obstacle, however great, standing in the way of the Kingdom of God, he is to go into the battle against it in the rooted assurance that in so doing he is allying himself with the will of God, and the firm reliance that God will support and reinforce him by His providence and His Spirit. He is not to prostrate himself before the mountain as if it were an expression of the will of God, and trust to God to overrule the mountain for good; he is to seek to explode the mountain and clear it away, by asking great things from God and expecting great things of God.

Are the words really capable of any other meaning? But if it be so, then, clearly, faith of this kind carries in its heart rebellion against the natural course of events, and this again carries with it the irresistible conclusion that there must be much in that course of events that is hateful to God. In other words, the whole of this type of teaching about faith carries with it a certain doctrine of the evil of the world.

It is clear that Jesus Christ conceived of the Kingdom of God as including in the first instance purely spiritual blessings—faith, hope, and love; but it is equally clear that it included also all that concerns man's sound physical life. It is impossible to believe that He who showed such solicitous sympathy for those diseased in body or sick in mind, those who were hungry, those who were in peril from the storm and the wave, could think otherwise of the Kingdom of God. But if it be so, then how did He regard that mighty course of events which is unrolled before us in human history? What view did He take of the presence of the evils that are manifest on so colossal a scale in the human story? Did He regard them as part of the unconditional will of God? In view of His many sayings about faith of this rebellious, creative type, I do not see how He could possibly have thought anything of the kind. The teaching about faith is rooted in a certain view of the objective evils of human life, without which it loses all its force and meaning; and it is largely because there has crept into our modern thought another view that the remarkable character of this teaching about faith has lost much of its vitality for us at the present time. That view is that the outward ills of human life, being caused by the physical environment, are due to natural law, and as these laws are unconditionally decreed by God, the ordinary evils of life are all to be taken as if they were due to the Divine appointment. This is, of course, simply the "closed system" idea of nature asserting itself under a religious form. A good example of this type of reasoning is found in the deeply interesting *Confessio Fidei* of the Dean of St Paul's. In this "outspoken essay" he maintains a true Divine Incarnation, in the person of Christ, but at the same time repudiates the whole miraculous element in the Gospels. "Still less," he says, "in my opinion, ought we to demand that He should break through the fixed laws of nature, which He Himself ordained, and in accordance with which He orders the course of the world. In so doing He would not have exalted Himself; He would have condemned His own creation."[1] It appears from this that it would have been spiritually unworthy of Jesus to heal organic disease, to still the storm, and to rise from the dead on the third day. The really noble thing would have been for him to recognise that organic physical disease, the whole realm of natural disaster, and calamitous and premature death were parts of the glorious Divine order. Now whatever we may say of this, it must surely be plain to every unprejudiced mind that it is in discord with the entire New Testament view of things. Further, it is in similar discord with common sense. Every sane human being in practice acts on totally different principles. He does not accept the ravages of tigers and snakes as part of the Divine order. Why should he have accepted bacilli in the body or the brain as such? Every normal human being prays for deliverance from accident by storm or flood, and still more from premature and violent death. This is a universal and natural instinct, and surely rational as well. Yet according to this passage all such prayers are for God's interference with "the order which He has made," and by such prayers the man is "condemning" God's creation. On what conceivable philosophy, moreover, the Dean can maintain that so mighty an intervention as the Incarnation is Divinely worthy and beautiful, while he condemns a complete Resurrection as unworthy of God, I fail to understand. Surely both are "interventions" in

[1] *Outspoken Essays*, Series II., p. 49.

the ordinary course of nature, or they are nothing at all.

The thought of an individual may remain at such a stage of thought as is mirrored in this *Confessio* for a time, because life is short and its intellectual, like its practical, problems are perplexing, especially when the mind involved is widely and acutely sensitive to the complex currents of thought of our age. But it is surely inconceivable that the thought of an age can rest there in its search for coherence and stability.

The perils of this conception of the outward evils of life as being part of the unconditional Divine Will for man become obvious in another paragraph of the same Essay. " The Divine Life, under human conditions, was the life that ended in the Cross. And it is worth while to remind ourselves that what is best for us is best also for others. The Church at present suffers as much from the vicarious hedonism of its social ethics as from the self-indulgence and greed of some among its unworthy adherents. Both are equally materialistic, both alike rest on an estimate of good and evil which makes the Incarnation unintelligible." [2]

The general drift of this, taken in connection with the Dean's other writings, is that Christ bore the Cross of the world's evil fate, and that this is the highest kind of life. If we would live the highest kind of life we, too, must bear the cross. So far we are all on common Christian ground. We are all under the vicarious law. But when the next step is taken, " the cross is best for others," we get

[2] *Outspoken Essays*, Series II., pp. 48, 49.

on somewhat dangerous ground. In part it is true. Historically, every human being has to bear his share of the common lot. But what selfishness and sinful apathy and cruelty that need not be may creep in and shelter themselves under that formula—" The cross is best for others "—however cultured, humane, and noble in spirit some may be who formulate it!

From this second proposition the Dean advances to a favourite topic, " the social hedonism " of the modern progressive party in the Church, which, it is not obscurely hinted, may be as materialistic as capitalist greed. Of course it may, but is it? And is its aim fairly described as " social hedonism " at all? It seems to me that the long delayed but gathering Christian protest against adverse social conditions has, at its roots, a deep sense of the sacredness and value of all human beings. Its true aim is not an increase in the pleasures of the poor, as the phrase " social hedonism " insinuates, but the assertion of their inherent right to conditions of life that will not breed disease, atrophy of the higher nature, unnecessary exposure to casualty, and premature death. Each and all of these aims seems to me to be as it were visualised in the " signs " of Jesus, and revealed by Him as of the very nature of the Kingdom of God, and therefore of the will of the Father. If this is hedonism, then Jesus Christ was a hedonist. But so is every one of us when it comes to dealing with our own children, or with any human being for whom we have real affection. What should we think if any one remonstrated with us for our solicitude for the physical and mental welfare of our children and for the provision of conditions essential for that welfare on the plea that it is the highest calling of our children to bear the Cross, that if that life was good enough for the Son of God, it is good enough for them? The truth is that in such reasoning we are moving in a sphere quite remote from reality.

But to turn from a writer to whose genius we are deeply indebted in other spheres of thought and practice, does not the conviction that the miseries of human life are unconditional and irremediable enter deeply into much of the higher thought of our age? I have quoted Huxley and Bertrand Russell as representative of the agnostic thought of their time. But have things been so much better with the thoroughgoing Idealists?

As I read Mr Bosanquet's account, for instance, of Religion, or Mr Bradley's account of the Absolute, I find that while morality is the region in which I am to strive continually for social progress, it is in Religion or Philosophy that I am supposed to rise into a region in which the contradictions and tragedies of life are transcended. I get "above the battle," and see that all things have their place, the lower and the higher, the real and the less real, in the Absolute. I am reminded of the well-known passage in a greater master from whom the disciples derive much of their inspiration.

"All the various peoples feel that it is in the religious consciousness that they possess truth, and they have always regarded religion as constituting the true Sabbath of their life. Whatever awakens in us doubt and fear, all sorrow, all care, all the limited interests of finite life, we leave behind on the shores of time; and as from the highest peak of a mountain, far away from all definite view of what is earthly, we look down calmly on all the limitations of the landscape, and of the world, so with the spiritual eye man, lifted out of the hard realities of this actual world, contemplates it as having only the semblance of existence, which, seen from this pure region bathed in the beams of the spiritual sun, merely reflects back its shades of colour, its varied tints and lights softened away into eternal rest. In this region of spirit flow the streams of forgetfulness from which Psyche drinks, and in which she drowns all sorrow, while the dark things of this life are softened away into a dream-like vision, and become transfigured until they are a mere framework for the brightness of the eternal."[3]

That is, assuredly, a fine passage containing truth that we deeply need to know. Religion is "the sabbath of the spirit," and we see nothing truly until we see it "under the form of Eternity." But deep as is the thought, is there not more than a trace of opium in it? One cannot but remember that Karl Marx began his pilgrimage as an enthusiastic disciple of Hegel. Is it surprising that if this was his conception of religion, his passionate hatred of oppression, his sense of the wrongs of the poor made him discard it altogether, and that all over Europe to-day his disciples in turn are proclaiming with a myriad voices that religion is mere "dope"? It is impossible to get

[3] Hegel's *Philosophy of Religion*, Eng. Tr., vol. 1 p. 3.

the Hebrew prophets into Hegel's account of religion, nor, it seems to me, is it any more possible to get into it the deeper and humaner mind of Jesus of Nazareth; and an account of religion that cannot hold these seems to me too narrow. Christian thought cannot admit of a God so wholly "above the battle." There is surely no room or ground here for the "faith" of which Jesus mainly speaks. Is there room for more than that kind of acquiescent faith which trustfully accepts the course of things because it believes that all contradictions are for ever solved in the Absolute, and that our highest life is to get "above the battle" too?

I gladly admit that many who have found their main intellectual inspiration here have been what Heine claimed to have been, and that they may justly be called "brave soldiers in the warfare of the liberation of humanity." But did they get their inspiration from that conception of the Absolute, or from an older tradition in which they were reared?

The real drift of this form of idealism, so far as its philosophy of religion is concerned, seems to me to find much more congenial expression in Hegel's notorious acceptance of the Prussian State of his day as the ideal and final form of human government, than in the passion for social reform of some of his followers, from Marx and Lassalle onwards.

Is not the root of the whole error, for such I cannot but believe it to be, found in the belief that the tragedy of human life is unconditional and immovable, and in the fatal readiness of even the best human beings to put the evils that confront them straightway into that category? In that case the only escape is to ignore them as unreal and illusory. I have been quoting agnostic and idealistic philosophy to illustrate this point, but what could not be said in like terms of the story of the Christian Church?

Modern history alone can furnish us with many examples. Why was it that the Protestant Churches at the Reformation were so slow in attempting the conversion of the world? They accepted heathendom as a great immovable mountain in the way of the Kingdom of God. They further acquiesced in it as the sovereign will of God, which it was obviously foolish and impious to oppose. Luther himself, who had taught such great things about the power of faith, took this view, and took refuge in the thought that the Lord would dispose of heathendom and "the Turk" at His second coming in glory and power. About two hundred years passed before evangelical Christendom began to realise that this was a mere opiate for the heart and conscience, and that it was not the will of God that the majority of the human race should live and die without the Gospel. But it took another century and all the momentum of the Evangelical Revival before the world mission of Protestantism got definitely under weigh, and it took a man of heroic mould to lead the more earnest Christian men and women of his time to pass over from acquiescent to creative faith. It is very significant that William Carey began his enterprise by stating his two famous principles,

"Expect great things from God: attempt great things for God." Something had obviously occurred to change his thought of God, to make it greater and more generous in this matter than Luther's. That development in his idea of God changed the faith of acquiescence into rebellious faith, and in the light of that he learned to look upon the gloom and evil of heathendom as removable, and to expect the Divine help in his attack upon it. Had he been able to anticipate the method of dealing with evil suggested by Hegel, he might have lived a much more peaceful life; but Christian history would have been very different.

If we come a little further down in history, the struggle for the abolition of slavery begins. Again, Wilberforce finds the Christianity of his day practising an acquiescent faith, and tolerating all "the horrors of the middle passage" on the plea that negroes were inheritors of "the curse of Canaan"; in other words, throwing the responsibility for the irrevocable judgments of God on an accursed race. We know how, even after his conversion, the devout Newton continued for a time to command a slave-ship. But the leaven of the Revival had penetrated more deeply into the little group of Abolitionists, and Wilberforce, and a greater and more generous thought of God was stirring within them, which gave them courage to pass beyond acquiescent to creative faith, and to sweep away instead of bowing down before the "mountain," or drugging themselves with thoughts of its "unreality."

The years pass on, and the progress of the Industrial Revolution fills the new factories with white serfs and child toilers. In the struggle against the evils of the new economic movement religious opinion was divided. The Hammonds, in their striking book on *The Town Labourer*, have put the two different interpretations which divided the Evangelicals as follows:

"The devout Christian, confronted with the spectacle of wrong and injustice, may draw either of two contrary conclusions. In the eyes of his religion the miner or weaver is just as important as the landlord or the cotton lord. Clearly, then, one will argue, it is the duty of a Christian State to prevent any class, however poor, and however trivial its place in the world may seem to be, from sinking into degrading conditions of life. Every soul is immortal, and the consequences of ill-treatment and neglect in the brief day of its life on earth will be unending. If, therefore, society is so organised as to impose such conditions on any class, the Christian will demand the reform of its institutions. For such minds Christianity provides a standard by which to judge government, the industrial and economic order, the life of society, the way in which it distributes wealth and opportunities. This was the general standpoint of such a man as Lord Shaftesbury. But some minds draw a different moral from the equality that Christianity teaches. Every human soul is a reality, but the important thing about a human soul is its final destiny, and that destiny does not depend on the circumstances of this life. The world has been created on a plan of apparent injustice by a Providence that combined infinite power with infinite compassion. The arrangements that seem so capricious. are really the work of that Power. But the same Power has given to the men and women who seem to live in such bitter and degrading surroundings an escape from its cares by the exercise of their spiritual faculties. . . . Thus, whereas one man looking out on the chaos of the world calls for reform, the other calls for contemplation: one says, 'Who could tolerate such injustice?' the other says, 'Who would not rejoice that there is another world?'"[4]

The nerve of the difference here, clearly, is that whereas the former view holds that the evil state of human society is of human wrong-doing and is therefore removable by the help of Almighty God, and calls for creative faith, the latter holds that in the last resort the evil state of society is due to the appointment of Providence, is therefore unconditional, and calls only for the faith of acquiescence.

The torch of progress fell from the hands of those Evangelicals who held the latter view and was carried on by Shaftesbury in the great career which reached its climax at last in the passing of the Factory Acts.

It is impossible and needless to follow the story all the way through, or to give more than one further illustration. To-day by far the greatest of all public questions is the question of the prevention of war, and the unifying of the nations in the common enterprise of humanity. It surely throws a flood of light on the prevailing religious teaching and thought of our time that all over the great

[4] *The Town Labourer*, pp. 223, 224.

camps of the British army in France the chief difficulty of belief of thoughtful men was the difficulty of "God and the war." How could one possibly reconcile the goodness of God with the existence of the horrors in which they were living? It was always, that is to say, taken for granted that God was responsible for the war. Just as it was in each of the cases cited above, the acceptance of heathendom, of "the horrors of the middle passage," and of the white slavery of early industrialism, so with many is it still with regard to war. Piety of a certain type regards this supposed Divine decree with trembling, but acquiescent, faith. Like Calvin, with reference to Divine predestination, it would say, "I confess that the decree makes me shudder, nevertheless it is true." Now, two sinister consequences inevitably follow from this belief. First of all, if we must throw the ultimate responsibility for the horror of the war upon God, the whole thought of God becomes darkened, and faith in Him becomes by so much the more difficult for those who still cling to it; while in many it is completely destroyed. Secondly, all those who hold this belief are thrown out of action for all hopeful and constructive labour for enduring peace. The belief that God decrees war must inevitably tend to make war inevitable. Surely the way of rebellious rather than of acquiescent faith is the way of Jesus. To Him who healed the sick it cannot be a matter of Divine decree that men should maim and torture each other; to Him who raised the son of the widow of Nain and gave the youth back to his mother, and wept by the grave of Lazarus for human sorrow ere He revealed the "glory of God" by restoring him to the home of Bethany, it cannot be a matter of absolute Divine decree that ten millions of the youth of Europe should be lying in early graves, and that for so many homes the lights have gone out.

If He really wrought those deeds, if they were characteristic of His mind and revealed His Father, then this is no case for acquiescent, but one rather for rebellious and creative faith, the faith which says, "War is an evil thing, it has no deep roots in the Divine nature of things, it is an intruder in God's world and it must be driven out and destroyed."

But the course of our argument has now brought us to the very heart of our problem.

What is the general view of the outer evil of the world, the tragic element in human experience caused by man's subjection to the material environment, that has been implicit all along in our argument, and that is now emerging into clearer light? I would say, to begin with, that the view towards which, in my view, the argument leads, is grounded in the best modern Theistic thought. It assumes that thought, and, starting from it, goes a stage beyond it, still, I think, developing its fundamental principles. First of all let us make that general Theistic position clear to our own minds. In general it may be stated thus. The world is a place of soul making. The supreme end is the creation and development of personalities. It may have other ends, but the final key to the whole is found in the ideal values, and in the spirit of man in which these are expressed and God is revealed.

From this standpoint modern Theism is able to show reason and meaning, too, in the hard schooling of man by Nature. We can show to-day with something approaching demonstration that not only man's physical being but his intelligence was developed in the struggle for existence, that conceptual thinking itself, as well as scientific thought is, historically, largely due to the pressure of the environment, and to the advantages which better ways of thinking gave to those who discovered and practised them. It was because men paid so dearly for their ignorance that they first learned to love wisdom.

The same stern schooling drove them into social groups, kept them there and taught them to discover and develop new ways of living that made society more secure and more progressive. There is no great virtue that dignifies human nature that has not a history, and behind that history there is always that same remorseless, insistent pressure of the environment. Religion itself has a history as well as intelligence and morality. A vital impulse like that which "first drove living creatures from the water to the land, and from the land to the air," and sent man voyaging from the arctic to the tropic zones, has prompted him alone of all living things to cast his life out into the unseen and the intangible, in quest of succour and at last of life everlasting. Behind that, too, we see the pressure of the dark, ambiguous natural environment, and of sorrow, suffering, and death—in a word, of the whole tragic element in human experience. Religion cannot be completely contained within any single definition, but assuredly always at the heart of it there is the endeavour to "overcome the world." It is "a prayer for life." It is a protest and appeal to the Eternal against the sorrows, sufferings, and indignities of the world of time. In the flood of light which the Science of Religion has cast on its historical nature the whole Communist theory of religion as "dope" disappears as a complete perversion of facts. Its roots lie, not in the desire of the mighty to drug the masses, but in the vital revolt of personality against the tragic element in experience. One of the great elements in the rise and development of religion has been death itself, death which has aroused the human spirit from animal acquiescence in its doom and sent it on the quest for immortality. Such is the general argument of the best Theistic thought to-day. Far from finding anything in the ultimate nature of the universe inconsistent with the Divine Love, it finds in that Love alone the true impulse and motive of Creation. Love is essentially creative, and we are really living in the heart of a great creative process, and witnessing the bringing into being of free human personalities and their education, discipline, and development.

The whole theistic conception has thus been wrought out with a breadth and thoroughness that in my judgment make it stronger and more satisfying than it ever has been before, and that make it, also, the most reasonable solution of the problem of Nature and Personality in the field to-day.

The argument of this book, indeed, rests upon this common Theistic ground and only proposes to carry it a stage further.

It is part of that conception that the whole outward world of evil which humanity has to undergo, the whole tragic ascendancy of the material over the spiritual, out of which so many individual tragic experiences come—outward accident, plague, famine, premature death of all kinds, and countless disasters of fortune and frustrations of toil by the niggardliness of Nature—are all in the Divine counsel educative and creative of knowledge and of virtue, of all in short that goes to make a full human personality. I do not, of course, mean that this is true of each individual. Calamities may happen to him that, being what he is, he cannot at the time surmount, falling on him not by his own fault, but by the working of the vicarious law. But the general principle is as I have stated it. Now it would seem, naturally and logically, to follow from this general principle that none of these evils are unconditionally fixed and fated as part of man's inevitable lot, but are all relative to his imperfect and faulty development and are therefore remediable, and, ultimately, removable.

The penalties of every rational educational system are capable of being escaped or removed by the pupil's learning his lesson properly. The reason for their existence disappears with the ignorance or the vice which calls them into action. Were it otherwise they would, of course, cease to have any educative power, because with their unconditional continuance the motive with which they supply the pupil for learning his lesson or amending his ways would be withdrawn. Why should he trouble himself to do either when he must suffer the penalty in either case?

But the thoroughgoing application of the idea of divine education to human destiny by Theistic thought would seem to carry with it the thoroughgoing consequence that all the outward evils of human life are removable if we could find and follow the right way, and, as we have seen, the human race has progressed in knowledge and virtue just in proportion as it has believed in the removability of the ills of its lot, and has resolutely set itself to remove them. The standard philosophical Theism of to-day hesitates here in the application of its own fundamental idea; it is not certain that there may not be a tragic element in the very nature of things that is unconditionally fixed and fated for man, so long as he is man, and that is, indeed, due to his very finitude. But if that is so there must be tragedy in heaven, tragedy as an eternal element in all creation. Against this I would set forth the idea that all human tragedy is educative, and is meant to be finally overcome. In other words, I would submit that current Theism should here speak with a more consistent voice, and carry clear through its own fundamental faith that the material exists for the spiritual, and that the present ascendancy of the material over the spiritual is educative and transitional in the Divine intention.

If we thus make the Theistic interpretation of the riddle of the world on this point clear and consistent with itself, we shall be now in a position to test and, it may be, to develop it by bringing in the historical personality of Jesus. Have we not here, by the grace of God, a unique opportunity of discovering what the Universe really is? Here is the ideal man, or at least, as all Theists must agree, the man who, of all men, comes nearest that ideal. Shall we find that He is subject, just as all the rest of us are, to that brute material element whose dominance over the powers of spirit is at the heart of all the outward tragedy of human life? If it be so then I cannot help thinking that here we have a grave difficulty for Theism which will be all the graver the clearer our estimate of the uniqueness of Jesus. But on the other hand, if disease and death fled away before Him as the Gospels say they did; if the storm fell silent at His word; if by His creative faith He was able to dominate the powers of hunger; and if, finally, He broke the bands of death itself, then to me it seems as if here we have a supreme confirmation of our faith in the spiritual character of the universe, and a prophecy of the day when all "death and crying and mourning" shall have passed utterly away. If it be so, then these miracles of Jesus cast a clear and penetrating light on the whole dark mystery of outward evil in human life; they are not external evidence of the revelation, but part of the revelation itself. In their light all that is dark and mysterious in our outer lives, and in the life of humanity, falls into its place in that vast process of creation whereby God is making and disciplining human personalities, "bringing many sons into glory." Yet, on such a view, we do not fall into that error, which we have seen to be so fatal to human progress and religious faith, of ascribing the evil of human destiny to the unconditional decree of God. The existence of evil in the world is not part of the eternal Divine order. It is a transient element, and seeing it in the light of the Eternal, faith may say of it what a Father of the Early Church said of the terrible Diocletian persecution, " It is but a little cloud ; it will pass away ! "

Humanity has endured terrible things, it is true, in its long battle and march, but what treasures of hard-won knowledge of God, of nature, and of human life, what records of heroic struggle, of love that has not failed, of faith that has overcome the world, it bears with it as enduring results of that struggle! It is, as we have seen, possible to take a gloomy view of that " long result of time," to arraign the process through which it has been achieved, to use the light of the ideal which has been given us for other purposes in order to cheapen the human achievement, and accuse the great world of nature, and Him who ordained it, and thereby subtly to assert one's own superiority to them all. I do not think that we find that note in the greatest and finest spirits who, while they feel most deeply the sorrows of humanity, can most justly measure what it has achieved. Rather do they " glorify God " and His world of nature and the consequent result in man.

Let us hear St Francis as, worn out with physical toil and suffering, he draws near his end:

" Praised be my Lord God with all his creatures, and specially our brother, the Sun, who brings us the day, and who brings us the light; fair is he and shines with a great splendour: O Lord, he signifies to us Thee!

"Praised be my Lord for our sister the Moon, and for the stars, the which He has set clear and lovely in heaven.

"Praised be my Lord for our brother the Wind, for air and clouds and calms, and all weather by the which Thou upholdest life in all creatures.

"Praised be my Lord for our sister Water, who is very desirable unto us, and humble, and precious and clean.

"Praised be my Lord for our brother Fire, through whom Thou givest us light in the darkness; and he is bright and pleasant and very mighty and strong.

"Praised be my Lord for all who pardon one another for His love's sake, and who endure weakness in tribulation: blessed are they who peaceably endure, for Thou, O Most Highest, shalt give them a crown!

"Blessed be my Lord for our sister the Death of the body from whom no man escapeth. Woe unto him who dieth in mortal sin! Blessed are they who are found walking by Thy most holy will, for the second death shall have no power to do them harm. Praise ye and bless the Lord, and give thanks unto Him, and serve Him with great humility."

Man has paid a great price for what he has won, but what he has won has been worth it all. There is no indication that he is as yet at anything but the beginning of his day's work; and when one measures from what he has come there is no reason to doubt but that he will achieve incomparably greater things by the Grace of God. But I can conceive of no better way of arresting his progress than by assuring him that there are divinely appointed barriers to his progress in the subduing of the material to the spiritual.

What has come over religion that it has allowed science to get ahead of it here? What man inspired by the true spirit of science will set any boundary to his aspiration to discover the secrets of the earth and the heavens? Why should religion accept limits to the power and the love of God and the possibilities of prayer? Against all such limits set by man's unbelief stands Christ with His incessant call for faith. It is indeed strange that men should have been so blind to this, and to its far-reaching significance. We are afraid of His words, we try to minimise them and tone them down. But the truly significant thing is that the fear that man might make too much of them never seems to have crossed His mind. His one fear seems to have been not that the men of His time should believe too much, but that they should believe too little in the power over evil of believing, loving, and hoping prayer. If He were among us in the flesh to-day, would He speak in any different fashion? But if He did use such words to us would we not be compelled either to disbelieve them, or else to recast and expand all our thoughts of man, of Nature, and of God?

The malady of our time lies in its contracted thoughts of God. We think too narrowly and meanly of His Power, His Love, and His Freedom to help men. That is what the "miracles" of Jesus and His teaching about Faith mean. That God is more near, more real and mighty, more full of love, and more ready to help every one of us than any one of us realises, that is their undying message.

APPENDIX A

PRINCIPAL LINDSAY ON THE EARLY CHURCH

"BUT, coming to the heart of the matter, it seems to me that Christian Science is founded on a scheme of metaphysics which is crudely absurd, and has built upon that a faith, which, to my mind, is entitled to all respect. So far as Christian Science is concerned I fear it is impossible to separate foundation from superstructure; but those who are not Christian Scientists may do so. Metaphysics apart, what is the kernel of this faith? Is it anything else than this, that Jesus Christ is the Saviour of the body, as well as of the soul, and that He can heal disease as well as sin? The whole Christian Church of the first three centuries believed this most earnestly. It is in the Gospels, the Epistles, and in the whole of the earliest Christian sub-apostolic literature—in the very forefront of them. Church historians have ignored the enormous part that the ministry of healing played in the early centuries of the Christian Church. I shall have something to say about it by and by.[1] Meanwhile you have only to read Harnack's great book on *The Expansion of Christianity* to see its presence and its power. I am almost inclined to say, from the standpoint of Church history, that the modern Christian Science has set out on a quest after a lost faith—once a most real part of Christianity—and

[1] *Sc.* in class lectures.

has in this way satisfied a dumb quest of the soul which Church teaching has left unsatisfied."[2]

APPENDIX B

ST PAUL'S VIEW OF FAITH

I SHALL avail myself here of a summary account of the place of faith in Paulinism, taken from Titius's able and exhaustive work *Paulinismus*.

"From this it follows that faith is the decisive mark of the Christian state, and includes in itself the whole of the spiritual conditions of salvation. It would be hard for any judgment to be further from the mark than Wernle's contention that for Paul faith indeed stands at the beginning of the Christian life, but falls into the background in its further course; that as a missionary he was a preacher of faith, but that with well-established churches he brought in the moral demands without associating them with faith. Let one consider only how Paul, not only during his missionary labour, but also retrospectively, sets forth the rise of Christian faith as the decisive mark of the Christian position (1 Thess. i. 3-8 and ii. 10; 2 Thess. i. 3, 4, 10; Gal. ii. 16; 1 Cor. ii. 5, iii. 5, xv. 11; 2 Cor. viii. 7; Rom. i. 8, xiii. 11; Phil. i. 29, ii. 17; Col. i. 4; Eph. i. 15); how nothing lies nearer to his heart than the maintaining of the Christian standing in faith (1 Thess. iii. 5-7; 1 Cor. xv. 2, xvi. 13; 2 Cor. i. 24, xiii. 5; Rom. xi. 20; Col. i. 23; Eph. vi. 23); the increase of faith (2 Cor. x. 15; Phil. i. 25), and the improvement of

[2] "Modern Religious Difficulties: an Address delivered at the opening of the College Session, 1907-8," *College Addresses and Sermons*, by Principal Lindsay, D.D., LL.D.; Maclehose.

its deficiencies (1 Thess. iii. 10). So decisive is Faith, that according to their relation to it Christians are distinguished as believers from unbelievers (1 Thess. i. 7; 1 Cor. vi. 6, vii. 12-15, x. 27, xiv. 22, 24; 2 Cor. iv. 4, vi. 14 *et seq.*; Col. i. 2; Eph. i. 1), and are bound together by it like children of the same household (Gal. vi. 10). Yes, Faith forms the foundation of and characterises the new Messianic Epoch (Gal. iii. 23, 25), and all doctrines are therefore to be measured by the test whether they agree with the norm of faith (Rom. iii. 27) or make faith void and destroy it (1 Cor. xv. 14, 17; Rom. iv. 14). These high sayings about the power of faith are quite intelligible when one considers that every one of God's manifestations of His salvation are appropriated and preserved by faith. Upon faith and unbelief finally rest men's fortunes for grace or reprobation (Rom. xi. 20-23). The preaching of the apostle is a preaching of faith (Gal. i. 23, iii. 2-5; Rom. x. 8-14, 15-17). Through faith not only justification completes itself, but also permanent access to God (Eph. iii. 12), and also salvation (1 Cor. i. 21; Eph. ii. 8), while the unbelieving as such are together condemned (2 Thess. ii. 12). Through faith Christians are sons of God (Gal. iii. 26); all the promises become the property of believers (Gal. iii. 22; Rom. iv. 16). Through faith Christians receive the Spirit (Gal. iii. 14; Eph. i. 13), who in fact is called the Spirit of Faith (2 Cor. iv. 13). Through faith Christ dwells in them (Eph. iii. 17) or they are awakened with Christ (Col. ii. 12), and God works in them (1 Thess. ii. 13, *cf.* Eph. i. 19). According to the measure (and relation) of faith all usefulness in the Christian community and all gifts are determined (Rom. xii. 3, 6). It is the starting-point (Eph. iv. 5) and also the goal (Eph. iv. 13) of the Christian community. In faith its freedom (2 Cor. i. 24) and all its joy and its peace (Rom. xv. 13; Phil. i. 25) are rooted.

As faith is the permanent faculty through which all God's manifestations of salvation are discerned, so also is it the principle of all Christian living. The whole walk of the Christian on earth is a walk in faith (Gal. ii. 20; 2 Cor. v. 7). In addition to direct communion with the grace of God, faith reveals its activity, next, in the appeal to Christ (Rom. x. 12-14; 1 Cor. i. 2), and in prayer. Prayer, indeed, is never expressly indicated as a fruit of faith, but since the Christian's filial standing and permanent access to the Father are mediated by faith, prayer too must be rooted in faith, since it is only the carrying out of that filial right. . . .

To the summons to stand fast in the faith the passage in 1 Cor. xvi. 13 joins in the closest way, "Quit you like men, be strong." Manly maturity (*cf.* 1 Cor. xiii. 11; Eph. iv. 13) and the strength of the inward man (Eph. iii. 16, *cf.* Col. ii. 7) shows itself in courage which one shows towards opponents, a courage which does not allow itself to be moved by disappointments and sufferings. . . . This manly and heroic disposition is the peculiar work of faith. For in 1 Thess. v. 8 faith appears as "breastplate," in Eph. vi. 16 as "shield," in Col. ii. 5 as "bulwark,"[3] and in conformity with this prayer is represented under the figure of a fight (Col. iv. 12),

[3] Soden's translation of word rendered "steadfastness" in R.V.

as is so often done with the whole of life, and in particular with the work of evangelisation, which usage, indeed, has its very real ground in the facts. The specific work of faith referred to in 1 Thess. i. 3; 2 Thess. i. 11, can indicate nothing else than courage to endure suffering (1 Thess. i. 6f.; *cf.* iii. 2-5). Faith also leads to vigilant watchfulness and self-examination. It passes easily over, therefore, into a great moral force. Titius therefore sums up his whole argument as follows: "Thus, beyond all doubt, the Christian life in its beginning, as in its development, in things great and in things small is borne up by faith. This is true not only of the strictly religious, but also of the moral functions." "Faith works through love" and "what is not of faith is sin" (Gal. v. 6; Rom. xiv. 23). "But if faith in its origin is morally conditioned, and further shows itself morally active, it follows that in faith we have the synthesis of morality and religion. It appears in the first rank as the permanent means for man's appropriation of the Divine Salvation. It comes into being under the impression of unconditional dependence on the grace of God. Yet at the same time it is throughout, in its rise and in its progress, morally conditioned. Clearly, then, the conception of faith (held by St Paul) is better fitted than any other to give expression to the whole genius of Christianity."[4]

That this is substantially a true account of the fundamental and vital place of faith in St Paul's whole conception of the Christian life seems to me beyond reasonable doubt. In all St Paul's writings

[4] *Paulinismus*, pp. 209-216.

it is a basal principle that not only justification but sanctification and the mediation of all the blessings of the new covenant come by way of faith. Not a few think that this singular emphasis upon faith is a peculiarity of St Paul, part of his original contribution to Christianity. But in the light of what has been said on the teaching of Jesus there is surely nothing original about it. It is wholly derived from the "author and perfection of faith," and simply repeats the new emphasis on faith which He introduced. Original St Paul certainly is, but his originality comes in at a later stage. He seizes upon Christ's principle, and applies it with extraordinary freshness, boldness, and insight, to the new situation created by the death and resurrection of Jesus Christ, and the gift of His Spirit. But so far as I can see there is nothing said in his writings about the vital place of faith in the Christian life which his Master had not said before him.

APPENDIX C

R. H. HUTTON ON PRAYER

"In His (*i.e.* Christ's) sense, it is of the very essence of prayer that it aims at the establishment of the Divine will and the annihilation of all that is inconsistent with that will. It is not to God's omnipotence primarily, but to his spiritual nature, that Christian prayer is addressed; the whole purport of it being that the unity of the Divine Kingdom may be asserted and its laws established."[5]

[5] R. H. Hutton, *Aspects of Religious and Scientific Thought*, 1899.

INDEX I

SCRIPTURE PASSAGES

(*See also Index II on St Paul's Epistles*)

INDEX II

SCRIPTURE PASSAGES IN APPENDIX B, pp. 249–253

St Paul's view of Faith

INDEX III

AUTHORS REFERRED TO

INDEX IV

SUBJECTS

9